IQ PU

About the author:

David J. Bodycombe was born in Darlington, England, in 1973. Over eight years his creations have appeared in various magazines and newspapers, and on television and radio.

For five years, he was one of the games creators for the UK Channel Four programme *The Crystal Maze*. He also researched and wrote the questions for two series of the BBC Radio 4 treasure hunt game, *X Marks the Spot*.

After graduating in Mathematics at the University of Durham in 1995, David moved to Kingston-upon-Thames, Surrey, where he runs a puzzle and game consultancy.

Author's web page: http://www.qwertyuiop.co.uk/

By the same author:

The Mammoth Puzzle Carnival

Lateral Puzzles

Optical Illusions and Picture Puzzles

Codes and Ciphers

IQ PUZZLES

Devised by David J. Bodycombe

This is a Parragon Book published 2002

Parragon
Queen Street House
4 Queen Street
Bath BA1 1HE, UK

First published in the UK as *The Mammoth Book of Brainstorming Puzzles*
by Robinson Publishing, 1996

A copy of the British Library Cataloguing in Publication Data
is available from the British Library

ISBN 0-75257-432-9

Printed and bound in the EC

10 9 8 7 6 5 4 3 2 1

CONTENTS

INTRODUCTION

From the comfort of my armchair, I often see contestants in TV game shows performing physical feats of endurance over obstacle courses in the hope of winning major prizes. At the end of the day, they sometimes emerge triumphant, with every muscle in their bodies aching, sweat running down their faces, and they become proud owners of a sparkling new fondue set to boot.

This set me thinking. Why was there no cerebral equivalent? So this book, *IQ Puzzles*, is a no-holds-barred attempt to devise the most wide-ranging set of puzzles ever published. Each type of puzzle herein is designed to test different skills so that at the end of each Lap I hope you will get the same feeling of every muscle aching – though in your case they will be mental muscles. I call doing twenty wordsearches on the trot "monotonous" – if you would rather describe it as "exhilarating" then perhaps this book might be a bit too exciting for you.

The challenge to the rest of you (which I hope is the majority!) is therefore twofold – to test your knowledge of your specialized subjects whilst also coping with teasers from a wider range of knowledge. I read that humans only use 10% of their brain so think of this widening of your horizons as "a good thing".

The book is in two halves. In the first half, Round 1, we test your handling of words, numbers, visual observation, technical reasoning, and lateral thinking. Round 2 tests much the same skills, except that I allow myself the extra armaments of general knowledge and tactics. It is not necessary to do all of Round 1 before attempting the first Lap of Round 2 and I suggest you will find it more interesting if you alternate between the two according to your mood.

This book can be used in two ways. If you're a laid back, occasional puzzler then you will find the format suitable for dipping in at random points, with Round 1 providing quick puzzles and Round 2 providing more substantial challenges. However, I expect 90% of you will want a proper limbering up course to flex those mental muscles. So I have devised a competitive scoring system with which you can judge your progress. As you go through each Lap of the course the pace gets tougher. The puzzles themselves are not graded in order of difficulty, although there is a "Target to Beat" which goes up in value as time goes by, and the challenge is to do enough in each Lap so that you keep yourself ahead of this target.

In every Lap of the book (35 in all) there are ten puzzles. Each round has its own scoring system, described in the appropriate briefing section. At the end of the book you can turn to the grading page to see how you've done. This should give the competitive among you a final goal to aim at, to either call your bluff or prove your brilliance.

I hope you enjoy the book, but if it turns out that you are an undiscovered genius I'm afraid you'll have to go out and buy your own fondue set. Just don't overdo it on the first day...

ROUND 1

Welcome to Round 1, which will be especially enjoyed by those with a liking for unusual, devious puzzles. But it's not booby traps all the way – there are some traditional puzzles to make you feel at home.

In each Lap there are ten puzzles. These are graded from 1 to 5 stars in difficulty, with 5 being the hardest, although the one-star puzzles are certainly no walkover! The stars also represent the number of points up for grabs, so solving a five-star puzzle correctly will win you a valuable five points towards your "Target to Beat" score. Up to 30 points can be gained in one Lap. No points are lost for incorrect answers. Use the first page of each Lap to record your scores.

So where's the big catch? You only have 90 minutes to attempt the Lap. Yes, this is harsh but just try your best and you'll soon get used to the pace. At first the target scores are set deliberately low so you can afford to experiment with different tactics before things begin to hot up.

As you progress through the book you may find that you get better at the puzzles and that your score rises. Similarly, the "Target To Beat" we set for you to aim at also increases slowly. See if you can keep up the pace! You can chart your progress on a graph we have prepared for you at the end of the round.

The five different categories of puzzles in this round of the book are listed overleaf, together with brief descriptions of the types of puzzle each one encompasses.

THE CATEGORIES:

 VERBAL – These questions test your ability to handle letters, recall words and form phrases. Vocabulary can play a part in the harder puzzles.

 NUMBER – Anything number-based is permitted here. Some of the harder puzzles might use a little algebra, but common sense may get you further!

 VISUO-SPATIAL – Requires the ability to observe and move objects around in your mind's eye in two and three dimensions.

 TECHNOLOGICAL – These puzzles often ask you to predict how a simple, real-life mechanical model would behave.

 LATERAL THINKING – Sometimes the right answer can be discovered by thinking "sideways". If you see this icon, beware...

Keep your wits about you in this Round – I have a devious sense of humour but the clues are there if you bother to look out for them.

See you at the end of Lap 25!

LAP 1

Time Limit – 90 minutes

For each correctly solved puzzle award yourself
the number of points shown in the table below.
See if you can beat the target.

	VALUE	SCORE
1. CROSS WORDS	3	
2. MAKING A MINT	1	
3. IN THE BALANCE	4	
4. PICK-UP JOB	5	
5. PICTURE LINK	2	
6. ...AND REASON	1	
7. INTERSECTIONS	4	
8. CANNONBALL RUN	2	
9. LETTER LINES	5	
10. ALL SQUARE	3	
TOTAL (max. 30)		

TARGET TO BEAT – 10 points

The simple crossword below has had the letters A, T and two other letters removed from it wherever they occur. Complete the puzzle.

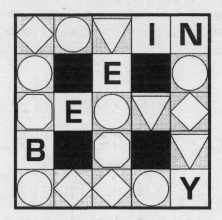

2 MAKING A MINT ★

Suppose you have an infinitely large supply of 2p and 5p coins and you wish to buy a packet of mints.

Assuming the shopkeeper doesn't mind the small coins, what is the most the mints could cost given that you are unable to give the shopkeeper the exact money?

IN THE BALANCE

★ ★ ★ ★

Place the weights given on the pans so that the entire system balances. The black numbers tell you how far apart each pan is from the next.

You can assume that the rods and pans are of negligible weight and can therefore be ignored in the calculations.

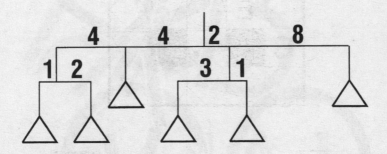

PICK-UP JOB
★ ★ ★ ★ ★

Which word do these letters represent? There is a logical sequence.

6

What is the common link between the diagrams shown here?

Why might these three words not be very useful to someone like William Wordsworth?

MONTH

ORANGE

ORIOLE

On the island of Lineus there are four roads which are completely straight. Where any roads cross there is an intersection, and on Lineus there are six intersections (as illustrated). Moreover, no matter how you rearrange the roads one finds that no more than six intersections are required.

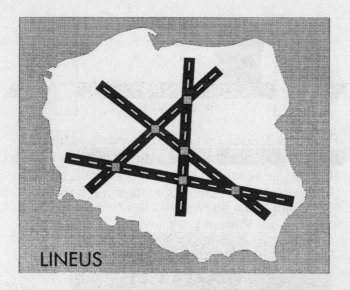

LINEUS

The neighbouring island of Lateralia has fifteen perfectly straight roads. What is the largest possible number of intersections you could expect to see on this isle?

A cannonball is fired and after travelling 5 metres it has reached half its maximum height. To the nearest metre, after what (horizontal) distance will the shot land? 14m, 16m, 20m, 28m, 34m?

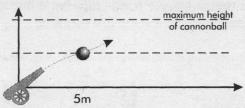

maximum height of cannonball

5m

9 LETTER LINES ★★★★★

Professor Muddleup has reordered the letters of the alphabet according to a verbal principle. The Prof has just realized that he has omitted the letter R by accident. Where should he insert it to preserve the logic?

A H B D W E F X L M N S

I J G K Q O P C T U V Y Z

Here are four miniature pencils, each one of which is two inches long. By moving just one pencil, can you form a square a little bigger than three?

(If you find this difficult, look closer at the question.)

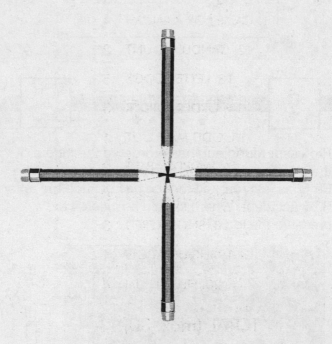

LAP 2

Time Limit – 90 minutes

For each correctly solved puzzle award yourself
the number of points shown in the table below.
See if you can beat the target.

	VALUE	SCORE
11. GAME FOR A LAUGH	4	
12. CANDLE COUNT	2	
13. LETTER COGS	5	
14. ORDER, ORDER	3	
15. ODD MAN OUT	1	
16. WORDS APART	2	
17. NATIONAL GRID	5	
18. SNOOKERED	3	
19. LIQUIDATION	1	
20. FILL-IN FUN	4	
TOTAL (max. 30)		

TARGET TO BEAT – 10 points

11 GAME FOR A LAUGH ★★★★

Although the phrase below sounds like something a hiker might make, the letters can be rearranged to form the names of a piece of sports equipment and two games pieces. What are they?
(They are all 6-letter words.)

THUMBED PROPOSITION

 12 CANDLE COUNT ★★

Since my birth I have always had a birthday cake, decorated with the appropriate number of candles.

To date, I have extinguished 253 candles in all. How old am I?

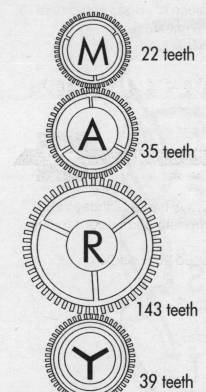

M — 22 teeth

A — 35 teeth

R — 143 teeth

Y — 39 teeth

The diagram represents four cogs which bear the number of teeth indicated. The letters on the cogs, read downwards, spell the word MARY.

The wheels begin to turn. How many times does the largest (143 toothed) cog have to turn before a four letter word is shown again?

13

Which letter should appear in the final disc?

Which picture doesn't belong?

Look carefully at the words in the box. Which word on the right could also be put inside the box to preserve the logic?

WEIGHING
MONOPOLY
REDEFINE
AUGUSTUS
ECDEMITE
TOMNODDY
OUTBURST

HANDBOOK

HEREUNTO

HIJACKER

HOBBYIST

HUMANELY

In an effort to design a foolproof system against power cuts, the UK National Grid is considering connecting every town directly to every other town with one long power line. The diagram shows that if four towns are connected in this way, six wires are required.

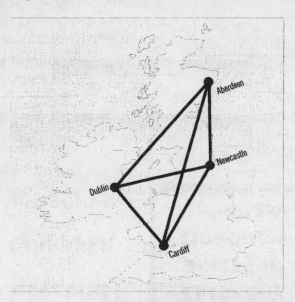

If there are about 895 towns and cities in the UK how many power lines would be required for this mythical scheme to be implemented? Ignore the complications of wires crossing over one another or over the sea.

18

SNOOKERED
★ ★ ★

A cue ball is fired around a 5 x 6 foot pool table. The ball is struck from pocket 4 such that the ball moves one foot vertically for every two feet travelled horizontally.

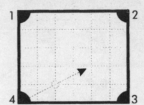

In which pocket will the cue ball end up, assuming it has enough power and the cushions do not affect the expected path of the ball?

 19

LIQUIDATION
★

A ballbearing is to be dropped into each of these beakers. In which experiment will the ball travel the slowest?

WATER	MILK	OIL	TAR
at	at	at	at
20°F	40°F	60°F	80°F

Work out the logic and fill in the missing square.

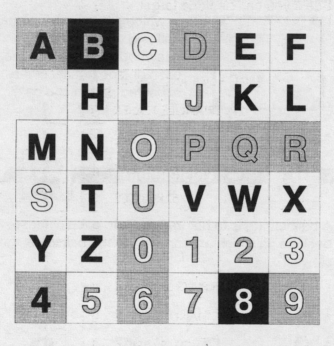

Time Limit – **90** minutes

For each correctly solved puzzle award yourself
the number of points shown in the table below.
See if you can beat the target.

	VALUE	SCORE
21. ROPE AND CHAIN	5	
22. TRIANGLE TEASER	3	
23. GLASS EYE	1	
24. DIAL 'M' FOR MYSTERY	4	
25. ROUTES	2	
26. DECAP	3	
27. PAT. PENDING	1	
28. SLEEPING SATELLITE	4	
29. HANDY RIDDLE	2	
30. PIN PICK	5	
TOTAL (max. 30)		

TARGET TO BEAT – 11 points

19

Place the letters on the rope and chain such that an English word can be read both clockwise and anticlockwise on the chain and the rope, giving four words in all.

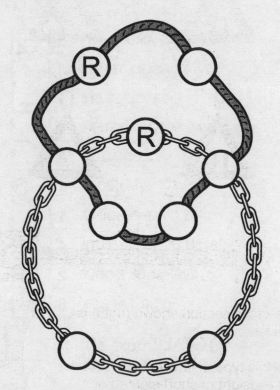

A D E F I P R R S

TRIANGLE TEASER
★★★

Which number should replace the question mark?

 GLASS EYE
★

The cross section shown (right) is of a lens.

Will this type of lens help correct the eyesight of short-sighted or long-sighted people?

My friend Jon has a telephone number that I can never quite remember, so I practise "dialling" the number on my calculator to get into the habit. As it happens, his number is 638468.

I dialled on my telephone to ring him last night but a voice at the other end of the line said "Hello, Newtown 692462".

Can you explain these events and tell me what I had done wrong?

Following the arrows at all times, how many different routes are there from A to B?

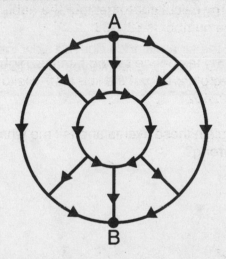

What special change can be made throughout this sentence to make the content rather more pleasant?

"Show this bold Prussian that praises slaughter, slaughter brings rout"

These two pendulums are just touching. Pendulum A takes 9 seconds to swing to and fro, whilst Pendulum B takes 15 seconds for one cycle.

Assuming the air resistance doesn't slow their motion down, how long would you have to wait to see them touch again?

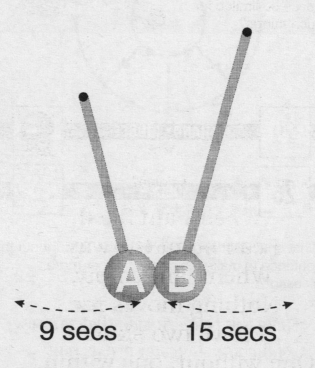

9 secs   15 secs

SLEEPING SATELLITE
★★★★

Scientists are concerned because in the future there may not be enough room in space to continue launching geostationary satellites. Why is the space so limited for such things?

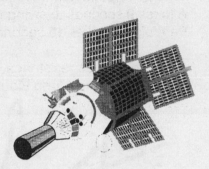

HANDY RIDDLE
★★

Can you work out this riddle?

"When I am filled,
I can point the way.
When I am empty,
Nothing moves me.
I have two skins,
One without, one within."

PIN PICK
★ ★ ★ ★ ★

Which pin is the seventh to be picked up in order?

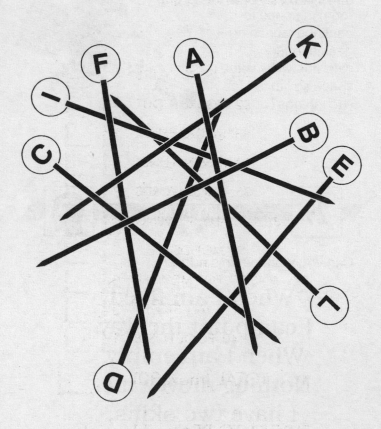

LAP 4

Time Limit – 90 minutes

For each correctly solved puzzle award yourself
the number of points shown in the table below.
See if you can beat the target.

	VALUE	SCORE
31. WORD INLETS	1	
32. FIGURE IT OUT	4	
33. SYNTAX ERROR	2	
34. MISSING LINES	5	
35. CHESS WORDS	3	
36. INITIALLY SPEAKING	4	
37. DIAMONDS ARE...	2	
38. MEASURE FOR MEASURE	5	
39. A TALL STOREY	3	
40. POOL POSER	1	
TOTAL (max. 30)		

TARGET TO BEAT – 11 points

★

Rearrange the same six letters to form words that fit the blanks in the story.

"Charles would _____ some of his friends to go carol singing, carrying _____-covered Christmas garlands. People would _____ as they sang ' _____ Night' "

★ ★ ★ ★

Five consecutive numbers have been hidden in the shaded boxes at random.

The numbers within the triangle total 27.
The numbers within the circle total 39.
The numbers within the square total 24.
All five numbers total 65.

In order, what are the five numbers in the diagram?

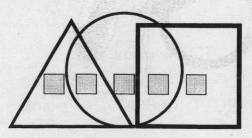

You may have heard the lateral thinking puzzle about the circus performer weighing 79kg trying to carry three 10kg gold rings across a long bridge that can support 100kg in weight.

The suggested answer found in most puzzle books is that the performer should juggle the rings across the bridge. This is not a good idea, according to which principle of physics?

34 MISSING LINES
★★★★★

Complete the last equation with one of the words at the bottom.

**SOAP = RISE
FLAY = CLOTH
CHAP = BURN
MANY = CAT
POOP = ?**

STRING   DECK   PALINDROME   MESS   NEEDY

35 CHESS WORDS
★★★

Can you find the four 11-letter words hidden in the chess board?

Prefix ten letters to spell out a word.

- CLEF

- SPY

- STRING

- BOAT

- MONTHS

- BOMB

- JUNCTION

- BEAM

- NECK

- LAYER

37   DIAMONDS ARE... ★ ★

How many diamonds, in total, are featured on the cards Ace, 2, 3, ..., 9 and 10 of Diamonds in a standard pack of cards?

38   MEASURE FOR MEASURE ★ ★ ★ ★ ★

The bottle shown is sealed but is partly filled with liquid.

Using only a standard ruler, how could you mathematically calculate the volume of the bottle without opening it or damaging it?

There have been many successful aircraft, such as the Boeing 747 and Concorde, which have gone on to set records for speed, reliability, size and length of journeys.

However, aeronautics has, so far, been unable to develop one sort of aircraft so that it can fly a distance greater than 2 miles despite considerable research. What class of aircraft is this?

How many balls are missing from this pool triangle, would you say?

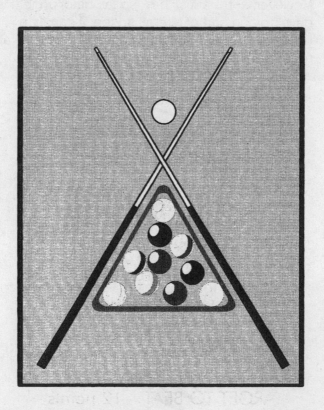

Time Limit – 90 minutes

For each correctly solved puzzle award yourself
the number of points shown in the table below.
See if you can beat the target.

	VALUE	SCORE
41. FOUR WORDS	2	
42. PRIME TIME	5	
43. IDLING ABOUT	3	
44. TIMELY MISTAKE	1	
45. SQUARE SEQUENCE	4	
46. COMPILATION	5	
47. MULTIPLYING NUMBERS	3	
48. EGGSAMINATION	1	
49. DOUBLE PUZZLE	4	
50. WORD NETWORK	2	
TOTAL (max. 30)		

TARGET TO BEAT – 12 points

Which word on the right can NOT be placed together with the words in the box to preserve the logic?

AURORA

BUREAU

COOKIE

IGUANA

ORIOLE

UNIQUE

UNITER

UREMIA

UTOPIA

42 PRIME TIME
★ ★ ★ ★ ★

There are 362,880 different numbers that use the digits 1 to 9 exactly once, such as the example shown below. Of these, what percentage are prime numbers? Round your answer to the nearest 1%.

2,654,387

The diagram below represents the cogs A, B, ..., I, J. Suppose these cogs have 36, 34, ..., 20, 18 teeth respectively.

Cog E rotates at 12 revolutions per minute.

How many times faster is cog J rotating than cog A?

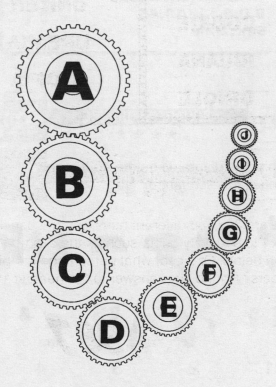

44   TIMELY MISTAKE
★

What mistake did this Russian spy make on his forged identity card?

IDENTITY CARD

Name : Steven Parchell
Address : 23 Arch St,
         Helsinki, Finland
D.O.B. : 12/10/46
Sex : Male

45   SQUARE SEQUENCE
★ ★ ★ ★

Which of the diagrams on the bottom row continues this sequence?

1   2   3   4

You'll have done many crosswords in your time, no doubt. Unfortunately I haven't had time to finish compiling this one.

Can you complete this crossword using six valid English words?

Hint – Most of our answers begin with B, L and R; a few more begin with J, N, S and V.

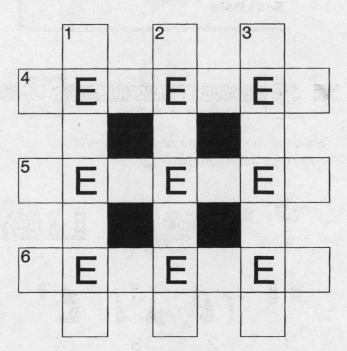

What number should come next in this series?

EGGSAMINATION
★

You have challenged your friend to an egg spinning contest. Whoever has the egg that keeps spinning the longest will win.

Your friend wins by a considerable margin. What should you check to ensure fair play has taken place?

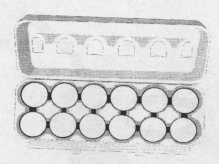

49

DOUBLE PUZZLE
★ ★ ★ ★

How many letters are there in the one-word answer to this question?

Spell out an eight-letter word, travelling along each
line once only.

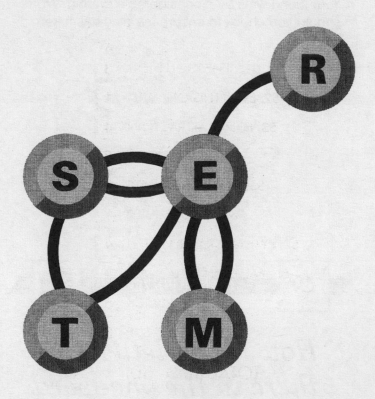

Time Limit – **90 minutes**

For each correctly solved puzzle award yourself the number of points shown in the table below. See if you can beat the target.

	VALUE	SCORE
51. SERIES SOLUTION	3	
52. EVEN THIS ONE OUT	1	
53. FERRAL ATTRACTION	4	
54. WORD CIRCLE	2	
55. IN BLACK & WHITE	5	
56. CODE BREAKER	1	
57. PYTHAGORAS REVISITED	4	
58. BALLOON BEHAVIOUR	2	
59. DRY DOCK	5	
60. SPOT THE SLIP	3	
TOTAL (max. 30)		

TARGET TO BEAT – 12 points

51 SERIES SOLUTION
★ ★ ★

Suggest a word that could correctly continue this sequence :

AID
GUESS
DEGREE
ESTATE
AVENUE
SENSE
?

52 EVEN THIS ONE OUT
★

Put 10 crosses in this grid such that there is an even number of crosses in every row and column, and in both main diagonals.

One of these pieces of iron is a bar magnet.
The other one is an unmagnetised iron bar.

Without using any other objects at all, how can
you tell which is which?

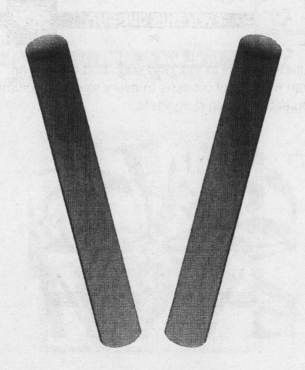

What are the LONGEST words that can be read in these words circles?

What word is this?

★

Using the clues provided, crack the code to reveal the answer.

1. Teacher
2. Printed bill
3. Fancy talk
4. Ticket-entry machine
5. Catholic minister
6. Adheres

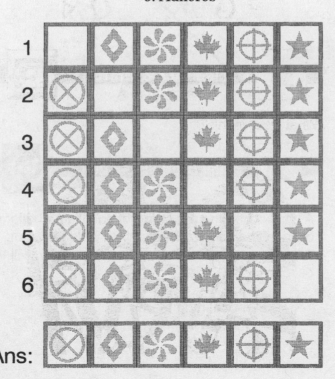

Ans:

47

Is it possible to construct a triangle like the one shown below such that there is one right angle, two sides are the same, and *a* and *b* are whole numbers?

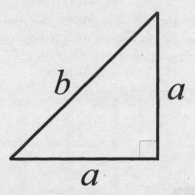

58 BALLOON BEHAVIOUR
★ ★

A child is holding the string of an inflated helium balloon in a car which has all its windows shut. When the car goes around a sharp corner, will the balloon :

    a) move into the corner?
    b) move away from the corner?
    c) stay still?

Lying in a well-known sea there is a ship that is worth many millions of pounds. The valuable ship completed its long haul to the destination but it was not able to make the return journey.

So the ship languishes there to this day and, although everyone knows where it is, no attempt has, as yet, been made to recover it.

What is the name of this ship?

Which of these diagrams is incorrect and why?

LAP 7

Time Limit – 90 minutes

For each correctly solved puzzle award yourself
the number of points shown in the table below.
See if you can beat the target.

	VALUE	SCORE
61. ONE WORDS	4	
62. BORROW 1, CARRY 1	2	
63. TOSS FOR IT	5	
64. PARASCENDING	3	
65. SPOT THE SLIP	1	
66. SIX ALL	2	
67. COLUMNADE	5	
68. PEN AND INK	3	
69. WITH/WITHOUT	1	
70. SQUAREA	4	
TOTAL (max. 30)		

TARGET TO BEAT – 13 points

What links these pictures?

Albert, Bernard and Claire have to share 23, £1 coins in pocket money between them so that:

i) Albert gets half of the total,
ii) Bernard gets a third and
iii) Claire receives an eighth.

"That's impossible to do with these coins," said Albert. "Not if Daddy lends us something," said Claire.

What did their father lend the children, and how much did they each receive?

This coin is not made of a uniformly dense metal. Five times out of every six it comes up heads, the rest being tails.

How is it possible to use the coin (as is) to give a fair 50-50 result?

James had just jumped out of an aircraft at 5000ft above hard ground when he looked up and saw a relatively large hole in his parachute. He did not use his reserve chute, no one else was around to help him, and yet he landed safely.

How come he survived?

Which picture is incorrect and why?

What is so special about these six letter words?

**ANIMAL
RECAPS**   **SPOONS**   **REPAID
DRAWER**

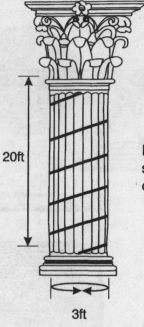

20ft

3ft

How long is the spiral on this cylindrical column?

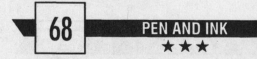

I am trying to write with my ball point pen but sometimes it works and sometimes it doesn't. Obviously the way I am using it is having an effect.

What am I most probably doing wrong?

The items above the line possess a certain property. The items below the line do not. What is the property?

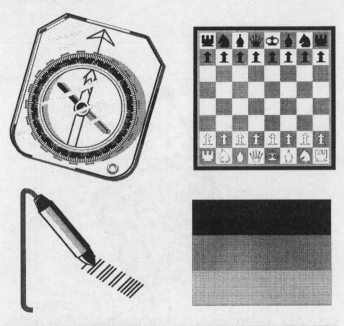

What is the area of the shaded square?

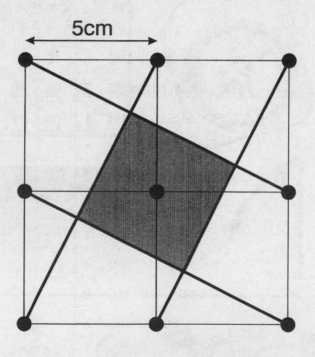

5cm

Time Limit – 90 minutes

For each correctly solved puzzle award yourself the number of points shown in the table below. See if you can beat the target.

	VALUE	SCORE
71. WHAT'S THE WORD	5	
72. RANDOM NUMBERS	3	
73. STEEL WHEELS	1	
74. HOLEY, HOLEY	4	
75. DIVIDE AND CONQUER	2	
76. GET IN SHAPE	3	
77. DRINK DEBTS	1	
78. PULLEY-OVERS	4	
79. WITH/WITHOUT	2	
80. ROUTES	5	
TOTAL (max. 30)		

TARGET TO BEAT – 13 points

71 WHAT'S THE WORD
★ ★ ★ ★ ★

What is the 12-letter word?

Forwards it is :
Rug; man; mother; B note; calorie

Backwards it is :
Plant resin; neutral pronoun; living;
what?; Scottish hat

 72 RANDOM NUMBERS
★ ★ ★

The letters from 'a' to 'y' are randomly allocated
the values 1 to 25 (a bit like algebra).

On average, what would be the result of the
product :

$$(a-n) \times (b-n) \times (c-n) \times \ldots \times (x-n) \times (y-n)?$$

In which direction will the big wheel turn if the wheel on the right is turning continually in an anticlockwise direction?

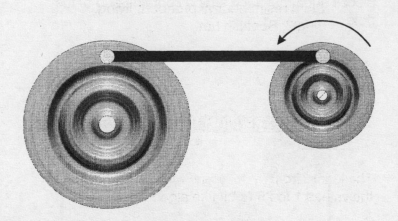

HOLEY, HOLEY
★ ★ ★ ★

There are several very good reasons for designing manhole covers to be round.

Name three.

75

DIVIDE AND CONQUER
★ ★

Split the shape below into identically shaped pieces such that each shape contains one of the dots.

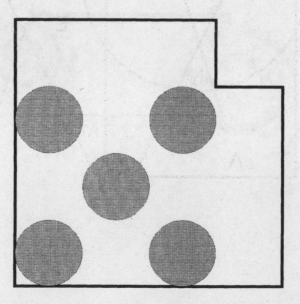

Which letter should replace the question mark?

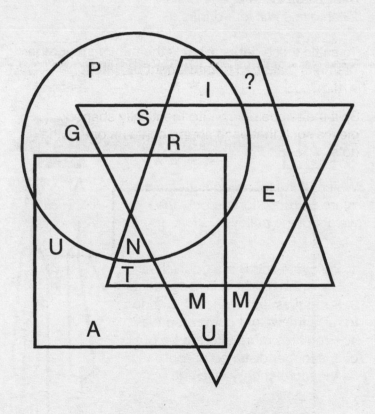

77 DRINK DEBTS ★

Four people are in a bar.
Wilf owes Xavier a drink.
Xavier owes Yves two drinks.
Yves owes Zillah three drinks.
Zillah owes Wilf four drinks.

To settle these debts, what is the minimum number of drinks that need to be bought by who for whom?

78 PULLEY-OVERS ★★★★

A   B

Which of the following statements is/are correct? (Ignore only the weight of the pulleys)

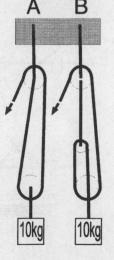

1. Pulleys A and B are equivalent.
2. B's smallest wheel is redundant.
3. B requires less work to be done to raise the weight compared to A.
4. A requires more effort to be put in over a longer distance of rope.
5. A is more energy efficient.

The items above the line possess a certain property. The items below it do not. What is the property?

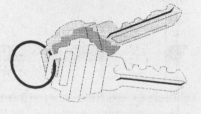

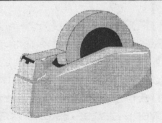

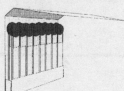

Following the arrows at all times, how many
different routes are there from A to B?

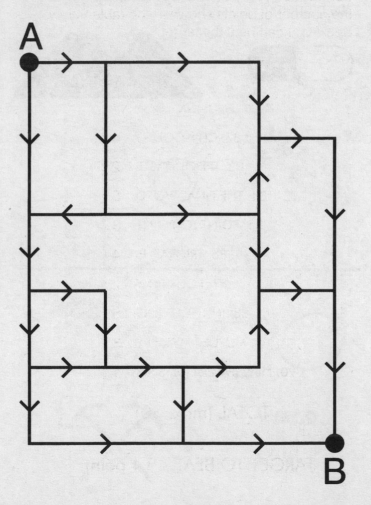

LAP 9

Time Limit – **90 minutes**

For each correctly solved puzzle award yourself
the number of points shown in the table below.
See if you can beat the target.

	VALUE	SCORE
81. NUMEROLOGY	1	
82. CHIP COUNT	4	
83. TRIPOD TABLE	2	
84. THE FINAL WORD	5	
85. POINT-TO-POINT	3	
86. TRIGRAPHS	4	
87. FOUR PLAY	2	
88. IN THE SWING	5	
89. MURDER MYSTERY	3	
90. NEWSPAPER NUMBERS	1	
TOTAL (max. 30)		

TARGET TO BEAT – 14 points

Arrange these in order :

LIVES SEAS

DAY WISE

CLOCK MEN

COMMANDMENTS

SENSES PACK

POSTER NIGHT

BED STAND

TIMING

82   CHIP COUNT
★ ★ ★ ★

At a certain Nevada casino, gamblers use $5 and $7 chips. What is the largest bet that cannot be placed using these?

83   TRIPOD TABLE
★ ★

A tripod for a camera is to be made such that on rugged terrain the feet can be adjusted to make the camera level with the horizontal. How many feet (one, two or all three) need to be made adjustable for this to work?

69

Complete the last line with a three letter word.

ANC ⟹	**NLS**
ESP ⟹	**AYN**
HCF ⟹	**TNR**
ICBM ⟹	**RLCE**
VSO ⟹	**???**

85 **POINT-TO-POINT**
★ ★ ★

What location can be read here?

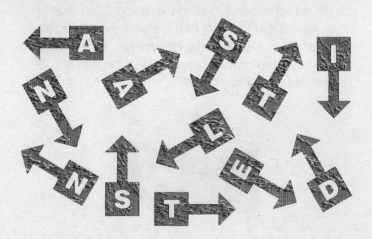

Can you complete the dashes to make five English words?

Clues to these words (in no particular order) are : baby, flower, Monday?, failure, indicator.

_ _ L T D _ _ _

_ _ G N P _ _ _

_ _ X G L _ _ _

_ _ F S P _ _ _ _

_ _ E K D _ _

71

87 FOUR PLAY
★★

What number satisfies the following condition?

"The same result is obtained regardless of whether the number is multiplied by four, or it has four added to it."

88 IN THE SWING
★★★★★

Ignoring the effects of air resistance, when will both sets of pendulums next touch simultaneously?

The pendulums take the times indicated to swing back and forth.

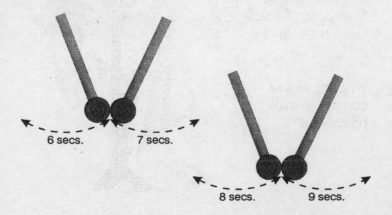

6 secs.   7 secs.

8 secs.   9 secs.

A man lies dead in a pool of blood and water. Upon inspecting the sorry scene one policeman suggests "It must have been murder and the perpetrator has taken the weapon with him."

A constable doubts this idea very much. "The door was locked from the inside, there are no windows or other ways out of the room, and there are no objects in the room. I suspect suicide. Moreover, I think I know how he did it."

What does the constable think happened?

My newspaper, which has a special 16-page feature in the middle today, is incomplete. The third page of the supplement (page 15 of the newspaper) is missing. What other pages must also be absent?

Time Limit – 90 minutes

For each correctly solved puzzle award yourself
the number of points shown in the table below.
See if you can beat the target.

	VALUE	SCORE
91. WORLD WORDS	2	
92. POST HASTE	5	
93. TYRING	3	
94. FORGETFUL = FATAL	1	
95. CIRCULAR ARCH	4	
96. SOUNDS FAMILIAR	5	
97. CALCULATOR CONFUSION	3	
98. BRIGHT SPARK	1	
99. AT THE STROKE OF...	4	
100. SPOT THE SLIP	2	
TOTAL (max. 30)		

TARGET TO BEAT – 14 points

What diagram fits in the final space? As is often the case, there is a clue in the title.

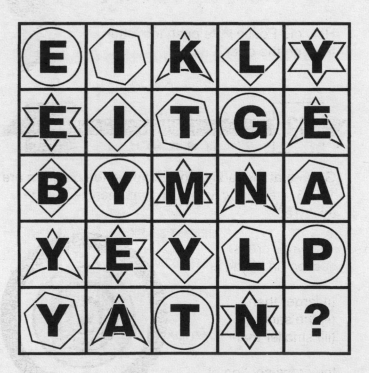

92 POST HASTE
★ ★ ★ ★ ★

Postie Pete has a square letter measuring 28cm by 28cm which does not bend. The letter is for the Robinson household but no-one is in to collect the packet, and the only hole in the locked door is 21cm wide. The hole is wider than it is tall.

How did Postie Pete push the letter through the door?

93 TYRING
★ ★ ★

Given that the radii of the circles in the diagram are 1, 2, 3, 4 and 5 units, which statement is true for this tyre?

The tyre's cross-section (in black) is :

(i) larger than
(ii) the same as
(iii) smaller than

the cross-section of the hub (shaded).

A lifeboat arrives on the scene of a catastrophe in the Pacific Ocean, about five miles off the coast of California.

A deserted yacht is surrounded by several dead bodies floating in the sea. What did someone forget to do?

The bottom of the ladder is exactly in the middle of a tunnel. The floor of the tunnel is ten metres wide. Can you tell us how long the ladder is?

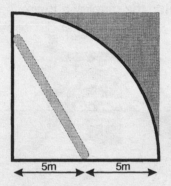

5m 5m

96 | **SOUNDS FAMILIAR**
★ ★ ★ ★ ★

What have the following words got in common?

BOW

DOE

RUFF

THREW

When I tap the following keys

into my calculator, the display shows :

I would expect this because :

12 + (one quarter of 12) = 12 + 3 = 15.

However, my father's calculator (which he uses for work every day) gives the answer 16. The calculator is functioning correctly and the same calculator is widely available for sale.

What is my father's profession?

A new six cylinder diesel engine is being designed. It will have a 1.2 litre capacity. The average speed of use is 2,000 revolutions per minute. However, the engine can only work at temperatures of up to 500 degrees Celsius.

How many spark plugs would an experienced engineer recommend to be put in the engine?

? 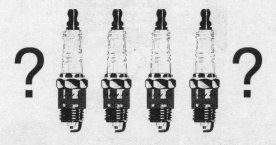 ?

99 AT THE STROKE OF...
★ ★ ★ ★

Add ONE straight line to make the statement correct.

$$20\ 10\ 5 = 4.40$$

SPOT THE SLIP

★ ★

Which picture is incorrect and why?

LAP 11

Time Limit – **90 minutes**

For each correctly solved puzzle award yourself
the number of points shown in the table below.
See if you can beat the target.

	VALUE	SCORE
101. START TO END	3	
102. TENNIS TOTAL	1	
103. BOX CLEVER	4	
104. THE POWER OF TWO	2	
105. IN YOUR AREA	5	
106. 21 POSSIBLE	1	
107. KING ARTHUR'S TABLE	4	
108. SPIN THE WHEEL	2	
109. FOUR INSTANCE	5	
110. KNIGHTMARE PUZZLE	3	
TOTAL (max. 30)		

TARGET TO BEAT – 15 points

83

START TO END
★★★

"A"

Complete all of the grids to form six common
English words.

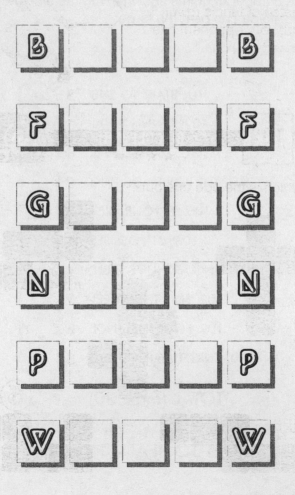

What is the least number of points required to win a "Best of three sets" match of tennis (given that your opponent has turned up!)

103

BOX CLEVER

★★★★

Which is the odd one out?

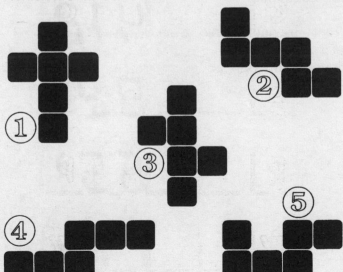

85

Which three digits
replace the question
marks at the end of
this sequence?

(Hint – try not to think
of these as three-
figure numbers.)

Here 12 miniature pencils (each 1 inch long) have been used to make a figure which has an area of six square inches.

Rearrange the pencils to make a figure which encloses an area of three square inches.

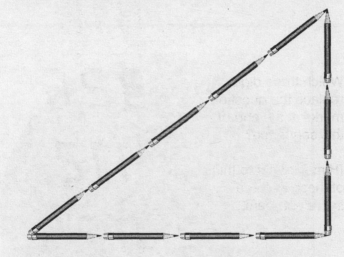

106 **21 POSSIBLE** "A"
★

What is so special about the following words?

NYMPHLY   RHYTHMS

87

The famous round table is in the corner of a room. It just touches a 5ft by 10ft chest of drawers as shown in the diagram below.

Therefore, how wide is the table?

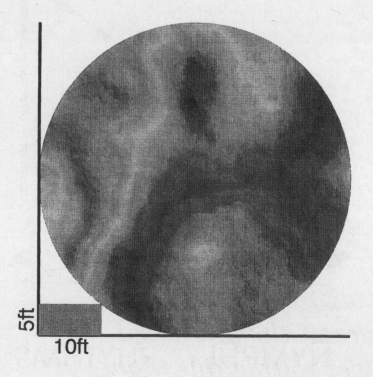

5ft

10ft

SPIN THE WHEEL
★ ★

Cog A, which has 8 teeth, is rotating clockwise at 27 revolutions per minute. At what speed is cog B rotating if it has 36 teeth?

8 teeth   36 teeth

FOUR INSTANCE
★ ★ ★ ★ ★

Where should Professor Muddleup insert the number four that is currently missing from the line-up?

Place seven more knights so that all 64 squares are attacked by at least one knight.

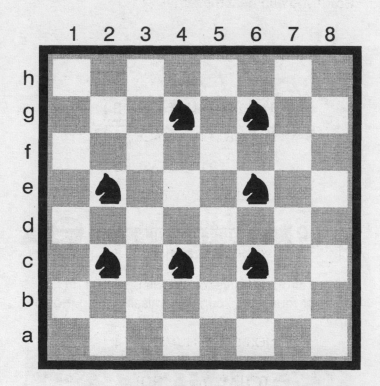

Time Limit – 90 minutes

For each correctly solved puzzle award yourself
the number of points shown in the table below.
See if you can beat the target.

	VALUE	SCORE
111. TRIGRAPHS	4	
112. TRIANGLE TEASER	2	
113. WATCH THIS SPACE	5	
114. AT LAST	3	
115. OBJECTION	1	
116. PICTURE LINK	2	
117. POOL PERMUTATIONS	5	
118. DRIVEN BANDY	3	
119. CLOCK-WISE	1	
120. NEXT-DOOR NUMBERS	4	
TOTAL (max. 30)		

TARGET TO BEAT – 15 points

Complete the dashes to make English words.
Clues to these words (in no particular order) are :
meeting, wood cutter, gossip source,
hold-up, office.

```
_ K Y J _ _ _
_ _ Z Z S _ _
_ _ _ P E V _ _ _
_ _ _ _ E Z V _ _ _
_ _ A D Q _ _ _ _ _ _
```

112 **TRIANGLE TEASER**
★★

What number should replace the question mark?
Hint – it's simpler than it looks.

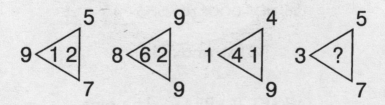

A man gets out of bed and finds himself in a strange place. He takes a coin out of his pocket and spins it on the floor. The coin quickly stops spinning and falls to the ground.

This was enough information to tell the man (a physicist) where he was. Where?

Which letter should replace the question mark?

? = 0.5
N = 11
D = 100
X = 6
Y = 20

115 OBJECTION ★

What famous object or landmark is this?

Can you work out which four-letter word you could best associate with the following pictures?

The diagram shows a triangle holding 15 pool balls. Seven are yellow, seven are red, and one is black. How many different ways are there of arranging the triangle such that each one is different?

Remember that a triangle can be turned through 120 degrees and look the same.

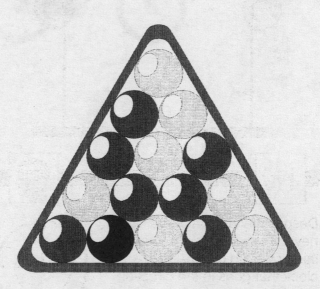

When the wheel on the left begins to turn clockwise :

     (a) The ball will roll to the left?

     (b) The ball will roll to the right?

     (c) The tray will stay level and go up?

     (d) The tray will stay level and go down?

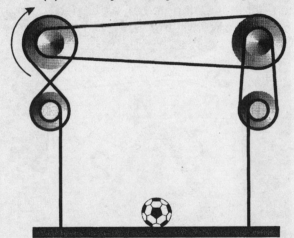

Despite the fact that there has never been a standard formally laid down, no culture uses a clock that goes in the direction shown on the right. How come?

97

Which number should replace the question mark to preserve the logic?

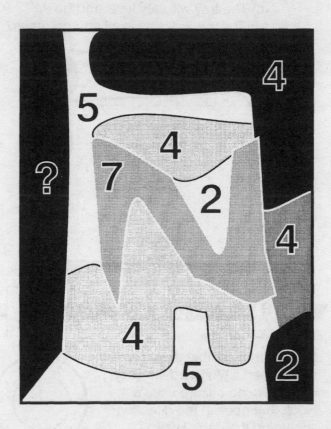

LAP 13

Time Limit – 90 minutes

For each correctly solved puzzle award yourself
the number of points shown in the table below.
See if you can beat the target.

	VALUE	SCORE
121. ANY WHICH WAY	5	
122. CHECK IT OUT	3	
123. BENDY BAND	1	
124. WORDY WISE	4	
125. RANK AND FILE	2	
126. PAIR UP	3	
127. THREE OF A KIND	1	
128. DI-ABOLICAL	4	
129. CRACK AWAY	2	
130. DICEDLY DIFFICULT	5	
TOTAL (max. 30)		

TARGET TO BEAT – 16 points

Which property do the following have in common?

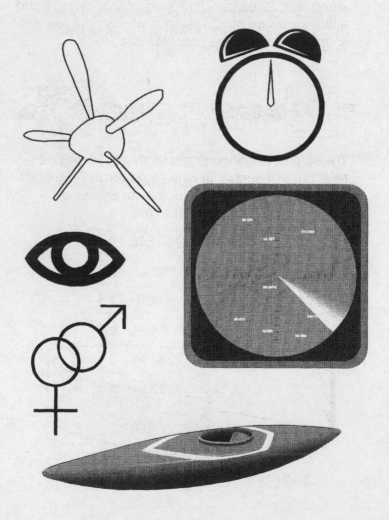

122 CHECK IT OUT
★ ★ ★

If you bought some CDs (costing a total of £27.80) along with 32 cans of lemonade, 88 postcards and a large amount of 12p sweets, why would you be suspicious if the total cost was £64.78?

123 BENDY BAND
★

The strip of rectangular paper shown has a half twist put in it such that when the narrow edges are glued together it forms a complete arrow.

How many (a) faces and (b) edges does the resulting construction have?

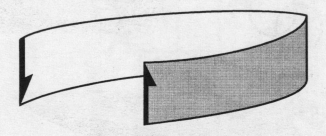

WORDY WISE
★ ★ ★ ★

What words are represented below?

ABCDEFGHIJKLM
ABCDEFGHIJKLMNOP
STUVW

RANK AND FILE
★ ★

Add stars, circles and leaves to the grid below
such that there is one of each symbol in every row
and column.

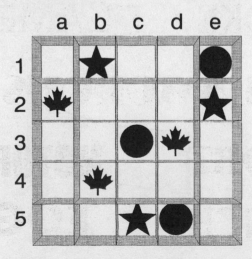

102

Pair these words together :

HOTEL   GLARE

CHUCKLE   RITZ

BREAKFAST

SMOKE   FLAME

GLAMOROUS

SNORT   MOTOR

LUNCH   FOG

Which number should come next in this sequence?

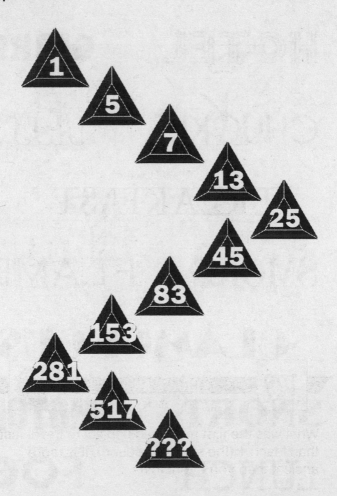

Which die is different from the other three?

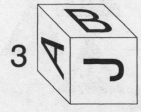

129 CRACK AWAY
★ ★

What was the first man-made object to travel faster than Mach 1 (the speed of sound). It is more ancient than you might think...

Here are two views of the same cube. Four of the sides have been shown between the two drawings. Draw the hidden fifth and sixth sides.

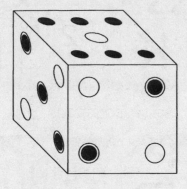

Time Limit – **90 minutes**

For each correctly solved puzzle award yourself the number of points shown in the table below. See if you can beat the target.

	VALUE	SCORE
131. WHERE FOR ART	1	
132. ACRE MONEY MAKER	4	
133. SYMBOL STATUS	2	
134. ANTIPODEAN ARITHMETIC	5	
135. SHIP SHAPE	3	
136. MISSING PAIRS	4	
137. THREE DIRECTIONAL	2	
138. AMBIDEXTROUS CLOCKS	5	
139. MENTAL METAL	3	
140. IN THE MINORITY	1	
TOTAL (max. 30)		

TARGET TO BEAT – 16 points

131 WHERE FOR ART ★

Which letter ends this sequence?

JRUOLMIEEO?

 132 ACRE MONEY MAKER ★★★★

An estate agent is selling four acres of land for £15,000 or seven acres for £24,000. He doesn't mind which offer people choose because he makes the same profit on either deal.

Today he sold 26 acres. How much profit did he make?

What does the following spell out?

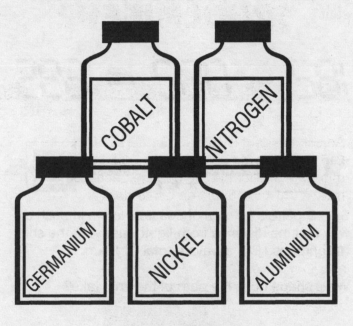

COBALT

NITROGEN

GERMANIUM

NICKEL

ALUMINIUM

ANTIPODEAN ARITHMETIC
★ ★ ★ ★ ★

By moving just ONE line, change the subtraction sum such that it is then possible to read a correct sum.

 $- 882 = 695$

 135 SHIP SHAPE
★ ★ ★

Ship S patrols an area of coastal waters in such a way that the distance from lighthouse A to the ship to lighthouse B is always a total of 10km.

What shape does the path of the ship take?

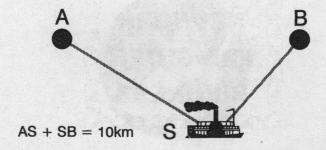

AS + SB = 10km

110

Which word below would be allowed into the box without destroying the logic?

ACERBIC

ACRONYM

AFFABLE

ANTENNA

ANXIOUS

ASSAULT

LIONESS

NETWORK

FREIGHTER

PUNINESS

What number should replace the question mark?

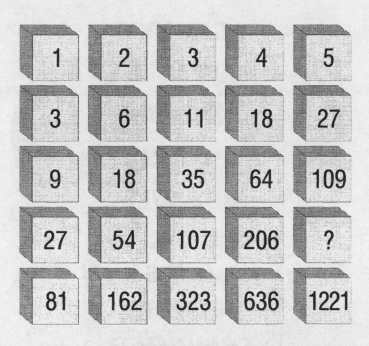

1	2	3	4	5
3	6	11	18	27
9	18	35	64	109
27	54	107	206	?
81	162	323	636	1221

138 AMBIDEXTROUS CLOCKS
★ ★ ★ ★ ★

How many times per day are the hands of a clock "confusable"? For example, clock A could be interpreted as either approx. 3:56 or 11:19, but clock B could only be 5:15 since the hour hand is in the wrong place for it to be seen as 2:37.

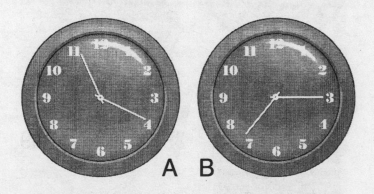

A B

139 MENTAL METAL
★ ★ ★

You have a tank full of mercury, measuring 10 by 10 by 10 centimetres. You also have nine steel ballbearings measuring 3 centimetres across. You drop the balls into the tank one at a time. How many balls will be completely submerged by the mercury?

Which is the odd one out in this group of objects?

LAP 15

Time Limit – 90 minutes

For each correctly solved puzzle award yourself
the number of points shown in the table below.
See if you can beat the target.

	VALUE	SCORE
141. ECHOWORDS	2	
142. SUM DIGITS	5	
143. HOT METAL	3	
144. COUNTDOWN	1	
145. CUBE COUNT	4	
146. NUMBER'S UP	5	
147. MANY NINES	3	
148. NET RESULT	1	
149. ALPHABET ADD-UP	4	
150. STAR STRUCK	2	
TOTAL (max. 30)		

TARGET TO BEAT – 17 points

ECHOWORDS
★ ★

We want to know what the seven letter word is.
The other clues should help you.

Express again

Land

Country

Gallery

Consumed

 **SUM DIGITS**
★ ★ ★ ★ ★

If you wrote out all the numbers from 1 to 15, the
total value of all the DIGITS you used would be :

1 + 2 + 3 + 4 + 5 + 6 + 7 + 8 + 9 +
1+0 + 1+1 + 1+2 + 1+3 + 1+4 + 1+5 = 66.

Can you work out the total of the digits from 1 to
999,999?

Suppose the metallic strip below is heated all over. Which diagram at the bottom of the page best represents the shape of the strip after heating?

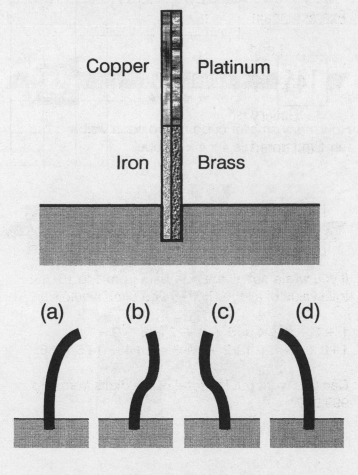

Copper   Platinum

Iron   Brass

(a)   (b)   (c)   (d)

Why do the "countdowns" at the beginning of old movies go :

10, NINE, 8, 7, SIX, 5, 4, 3...

How many smaller cubes have been visibly removed from this 4 x 4 x 4 cube?

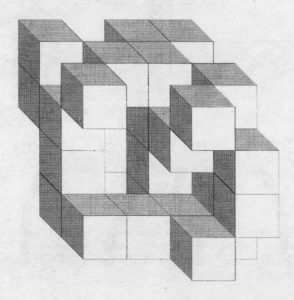

What would come next in this sequence?

1000

1,000,000,000

1,000,000,000,000,000,000,000,000,000,000

100

1

4

8

3

Note – In the UK the first number would be 101 and the third number would be a 1 with 48 zeros after it. The second number might also be different. This information may provide all readers with an extra clue.

147   MANY NINES
★ ★ ★

Some people think that the recurring decimal
0.99999... (where the dots represent a never-
ending row of 9s) is the same thing as 1.

Other people don't agree. They think "No matter
how many 9s you add, you'll never quite get to 1
exactly."

Which is right :
      (a) 0.99999... is the same as 1;
      (b) 0.99999... is not the same as 1?

148   NET RESULT
★

What object would the following shape resemble
when folded up?

What expression from those (a) to (e) at the bottom of the page would suitably complete the final equation?

HOB ✕ IST ═ Craftsman

UNS ＋ LED ═ Fallen

NON ＋ SED ═ Perplexed

AIM — LY ═ Purposeless

MIS — NLY ═ ?

(a) without
(b) with error
(c) withdrawal
(d) winsome
(e) winterwear

121

Which of the four numbered pieces is NOT used in the construction of the completed star-shaped cake-cutter at the bottom of the page?

1  2

3  4

Time Limit – 90 minutes

For each correctly solved puzzle award yourself
the number of points shown in the table below.
See if you can beat the target.

	VALUE	SCORE
151. A FABULOUS WORD	3	
152. STEAK YOUR CLAIM	1	
153. A BORING QUESTION	4	
154. ABLE ALEX	2	
155. MIRROR, MIRROR	5	
156. TOTALLY USEFUL	1	
157. TELEGRAPH TEASER	4	
158. BELT UP	2	
159. ON THE RIGHT TRACK	5	
160. MENTAL BLOCKS	3	

TOTAL (max. 30)

TARGET TO BEAT – 17 points

A FABULOUS WORD
151
★ ★ ★

Which word is suggested by :

"Midday starting block Last of the Mohicans second in command bottom of the barrel second guess at wit's end beginning of the end starting line early years"?

 STEAK YOUR CLAIM
152
★

Smorgers the Chef has six steaks that each require 10 minutes of browning on each side. He only has one pan, which can hold two steaks at a time.

What is the least amount of time required before all six steaks are brown on both sides?

A BORING QUESTION
★ ★ ★ ★

Willy the Woodworm plans to bore through as many wooden cubes as possible (from the 3 by 3 by 3 stack of cubes shown) by starting at one corner and going from cube to adjacent cube, ending in the middle.

What is the largest number of cubes he could possibly chew through?

Alex was once asked a very strange question in his science class :

"Was Noah good at biology?"

He didn't really know the answer, but came up with the right idea after thinking for a little while about what they had been taught last lesson.

What do you think he answered and why?

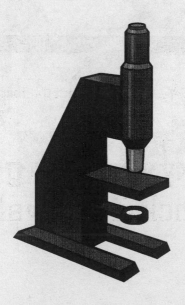

155 MIRROR, MIRROR
★ ★ ★ ★ ★

Continue the sequence for the remaining letters.
(The numbers are used for reference in the
solutions.)

1	A				M			TUVWX
2	BCDE			K				
3			HI			NO	S	
4		FG	J	L		PQR		

156 TOTALLY USEFUL
★

What is REALLY special about the following
sentence?

Foxy nymphs grab quick jived waltz.

A new type of indestructible cable has been put around the world to help the supply of communications. Unfortunately, 100 metres too much cable has been made. The engineers decide that it would be best if the cable is propped up by telegraph posts, as shown on the diagram (not to scale).

Approximately, what height would the posts need to be for this crazy idea to work?

158 BELT UP
★ ★

The cog on the right has a clockwise force applied
to it. Will the system have an :

(a) odd number of cogs turning clockwise;
(b) even number of cogs turning clockwise?

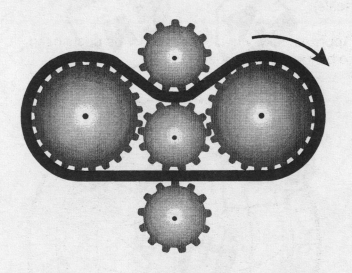

159 ON THE RIGHT TRACK
★ ★ ★ ★ ★

What sort of perfectly ordinary human being would
use their right leg to travel 20 metres farther than
their left leg on an average day?

What word do these blocks spell out when fitted together? (Guessers beware – there are over 20 different anagrams of these letters!)

LAP 17

Time Limit – 90 minutes

For each correctly solved puzzle award yourself
the number of points shown in the table below.
See if you can beat the target.

	VALUE	SCORE
161. INITIALLY SPEAKING	4	
162. A BAD GAMBLE	2	
163. CLOCK ON	5	
164. ROMAN RULER?	3	
165. PIECE OF PIE	1	
166. LIPOGRAM	2	
167. SPIRAL SUM	5	
168. IN THE SWING	3	
169. RETURN TO THE FOLD	1	
170. SYMBOL SQUARE	4	
TOTAL (max. 30)		

TARGET TO BEAT – 18 points

What eight-letter word is suggested here?

- **DAY**
- **BOAT**
- **BOMB**
- **SHIRT**
- **BOMB**
- **MOVIE**
- **NUMBERS**
- **RING**

When playing a deadlier version of Russian roulette against an opponent, three bullets are put into consecutive chambers of a six-shooter gun and the barrel is spun.

What is your chance of winning if you have your turn at pulling the trigger first?

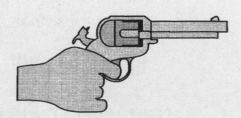

CLOCK ON
★ ★ ★ ★ ★

The readout below is from a 24-hour digital clock. How many times a day will the clock display a "palindromic time"?

(That is, a six digit number which reads the same backwards and forwards, such as 05:22:50 as shown below.)

```
05:22:50
```

"Five hundred begins it, five hundred ends it,
Five in the middle is seen.
First of all figures, the first of all letters,
Take up their stations between.
Join all together and then you will bring,
Before you the name of an eminent king."

Which king?

 165 PIECE OF PIE
★

How many circular pieces, each 4 inches wide,
can be cut from a pizza that measures 12 inches in
diameter?

This is the first sentence from the book *Gadsby*, by E. V. Wright. What is so unusual about it?

If Youth, throughout all history, had had a champion to stand up for it; to show a doubting world that a child can think; and possibly, do it practically; you wouldn't constantly run across folks today who claim that "a child don't know anything."

The diagram shows a spiral effect constructed with straight lines of increasing length.

So far the length along the whole spiral is 42 centimetres, using twelve lines. Suppose the spiral is extended so that 1000 lines are used. What would the total length of the spiral become?

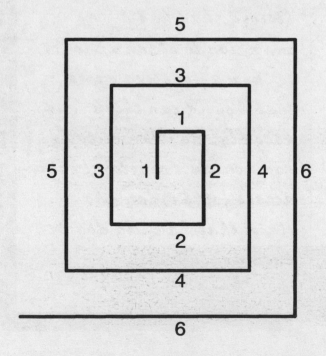

IN THE SWING
★ ★ ★

At the extremes of their swings, these two pendulums will just touch. Ignoring the effect of air resistance, when will they next touch?

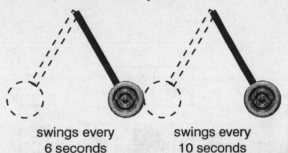

swings every
6 seconds

swings every
10 seconds

169 ## RETURN TO THE FOLD
★

Suppose you take a piece of paper and fold it in half to create two areas separated by one fold. You then fold the paper in half again, creating four areas separated by two folds.

Continuing in this fashion, at the rate of one fold per minute, approx. how many areas will there be between the folds in the paper after 20 minutes?

> *(a) 250*
> *(b) 5,000*
> *(c) 100,000*
> *(c) 2 million*

Arrange the tiles into the grid so that the lines read the same across and down (that is, 1 across is the same as 1 down, 2 across is the same as 2 down, etc.)

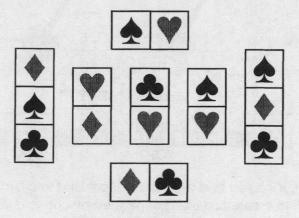

LAP 18

Time Limit – 90 minutes

For each correctly solved puzzle award yourself
the number of points shown in the table below.
See if you can beat the target.

	VALUE	SCORE
171. PICTURE LINK	5	
172. TRAIN TRIP	3	
173. STEEL WHEELS	1	
174. THINK SMALL	4	
175. ROTOBALLS	2	
176. PART THREE	3	
177. GET THE POINT?	1	
178. CUBISM	4	
179. TWO WOMEN	2	
180. CHESS COVER	5	
TOTAL (max. 30)		

TARGET TO BEAT – 18 points

What especially links the following pictures?

172 TRAIN TRIP
★ ★ ★

On a train journey, Barney the Boffin travelled from Birmingham. After a quarter of the journey was over the time was 3:31pm. When there was a third of the trip left to go the time was 4:31pm.

At what time did he arrive at the destination?

 173 STEEL WHEELS
★

These two ballbearings look the same, and they also weigh the same. However, one is made of a solid metal; the other is made from more dense metal and is hollow inside.

Without using any equipment, what is the easiest way to tell which one is hollow and which is solid?

174 THINK SMALL
★ ★ ★ ★

What special property do all these letters of the alphabet have?

C O P S V W X Z

175 ROTOBALLS
★ ★

Two balls lie on either side of a hollow, horizontal cylinder. The diameter of the cylinder is three times the diameter of either ball. Both balls are pushed around the cylinder until they return to their respective starting points.

How many more times will the outer ball turn through 360 degrees compared to the inner ball?

PART THREE

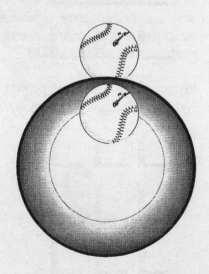

Name eight parts of the body that have three letters in them. There are at least ten.

(They must be proper parts – wax, lap, fat etc. do not count.)

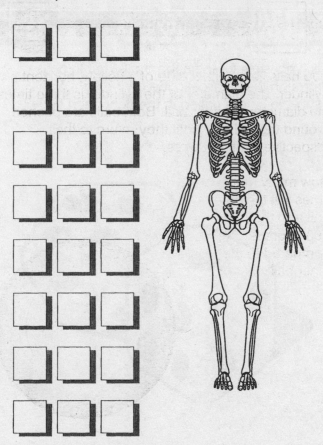

143

177 GET THE POINT?
★

Which three digit number, when multiplied by 4, is equal to 9?

 178 CUBISM
★ ★ ★ ★

Is it possible for the cube on the left to pass through the identical cube on the right if one suitable hole is drilled in the right-hand cube?

There are two women I know :

Deborah was born in 1973 in Cambridge.
Katherine was born in the same year, and
Cambridge is her town of birth also.

I know that both women have led perfectly normal
lifestyles and have normal eyesight and yet I am
99% certain that Katherine has never laid eyes
upon Deborah (even unwittingly) and vice versa.

How can I be so sure that this statement is true?

?

I have one of these chessboards and you have the other. We both have 21 triple dominoes shaped like :

Suppose we both cover our boards with the dominoes. This will cover 63 of the 64 squares on each board. What is the chance that we have the same square uncovered? (And, no, it isn't one in 64.)

146

LAP 19

Time Limit – 90 minutes

For each correctly solved puzzle award yourself
the number of points shown in the table below.
See if you can beat the target.

	VALUE	SCORE
181. WHAT'S THE WORD?	1	
182. POWER PLAY	4	
183. MONKEY BUSINESS	2	
184. KEEP ON ROCKING	5	
185. OUT OF THIS WORLD	3	
186. ALL CHANGE	4	
187. SYMBOL SUM	2	
188. RIGHT ON TIME	5	
189. QUESTION = CLUE	3	
190. WHAT HAPPENS NEXT?	1	
TOTAL (max. 30)		

TARGET TO BEAT – 18 points

181 WHAT'S THE WORD? "A" ★

Forwards, this word means "tense".
Backwards, the word means "puddings".

What's the word?

182 POWER PLAY ★ ★ ★ ★

This sequence doesn't seem to know whether it should be going up or down. Can you supply the next number?

The monkey and the weight each weigh the same amount.

The monkey begins to climb the rope. Will :

(a) the monkey and the weight reach the pulley wheel at the same time;
(b) the weight gets there first;
(c) the monkey gets there first?

Illinois Jones is being chased by a huge 30ft wide boulder – again. The rock is quickly gaining on him and although the tunnel is blocked, he figures out a way to avoid the boulder (just in the nick of time, of course). How does he do it?

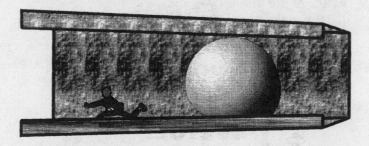

 185 OUT OF THIS WORLD ★★★

What picture should replace the question mark?

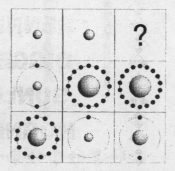

150

Which one of the words below rightfully belongs inside the box to preserve the logic?

GOPHER

EIGHTH

LENGTH

WOOFER

PREFIX

VETOED

GRUDGE

GIFTED

GRUNTS

RENNET

DIGGER

SUNLIT

HOGNUT

187   SYMBOL SUM
★ ★

What is the (usual) result of this calculation? Can you see how the trick works?

**((Last 2 digits of your phone number) x 2
+ your house number – your age in years) x 18.**

**Sum the digits of the result.
(If the result is not a single digit, sum digits again.)**

188   RIGHT ON TIME
★ ★ ★ ★ ★

How many times per day do the hour and minute hands of an analogue clock form a 90 degree (right) angle? One such situation is illustrated.

What number would logically come next in this sequence?

Work out where each square is travelling then use
the logic to complete the final picture.

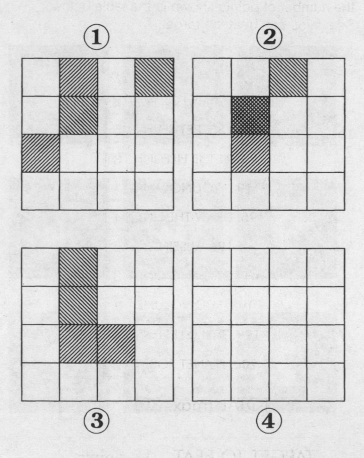

154

LAP 20

Time Limit – **90 minutes**

For each correctly solved puzzle award yourself
the number of points shown in the table below.
See if you can beat the target.

	VALUE	SCORE
191. TIME FOR A...	2	
192. SECRET SEVEN	5	
193. IN THE PIPELINE	3	
194. YOUNG MAN	1	
195. DRAW THE LINE	4	
196. MISSING...	5	
197. APPROACHING ONE	3	
198. FULL VOLUME	1	
199. TITLED LETTERS	4	
200. PLANET POSER	2	
TOTAL (max. 30)		

TARGET TO BEAT – 19 points

TIME FOR A...
★ ★

What could be put in the ninth box?

192   SECRET SEVEN
★ ★ ★ ★ ★

Imagine that the digit "7" has been banned from use for superstitious reasons. So what we would call "the seventh number" is now written using the symbol "8", the 8th number is "9", the 9th is "10", the 10th is "11", the 16th is "18" and so on.

Complete : The _____th number is written as 4685.

193   IN THE PIPELINE
★ ★ ★

Which arrangement of pipes will carry the most water?

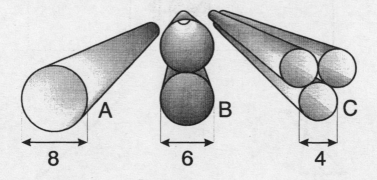

A   B   C

8   6   4

A man was born in the year 1340 and yet he died in the year 1322.

Using the normal calendar, how is this possible?

Which number replaces the question mark?

= 8   24 =

30 =

= ?   12 =

What links the following clues?

○ Place in Jordan

○ Middle Eastern person

○ Libyan leader

○ Foreign judge

○ Southern hemisphere national airline

○ State in Persian Gulf

○ Currency of Albania

○ Letter of the Hebrew alphabet

Which number comes next in this series?

0.5

0.6666666

0.75

0.8

0.8333333

Which solid has the most volume? The diagrams are not necessarily to scale.

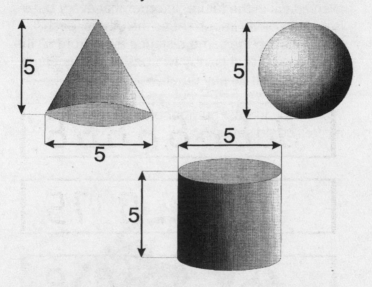

What is the significance of the following letters?

MOMMA OFT HOOK BETH
BORN SIZZLING UPSTREAM

The World Government wishes to place some military bases around Earth to protect against an alien attack in the future. In order that every base is seen to be as important as the others, each base must be the same distance away from all the other bases. That is, any two bases are the same distance apart as any other two bases.

What is the largest number of bases that the military could set up?

LAP 21

Time Limit – **90 minutes**

For each correctly solved puzzle award yourself
the number of points shown in the table below.
See if you can beat the target.

	VALUE	SCORE
201. MIDDLE ROW	3	
202. RUN FOR IT	1	
203. SIDE-SHOW SCANDAL	4	
204. SNAP	2	
205. DOMINO DERBY	5	
206. LENGTH MATTERS	1	
207. NOT NEXT	4	
208. GET UP STEAM	2	
209. FAME PILLS?	5	
210. WORD NETWORK	3	
TOTAL (max. 30)		

TARGET TO BEAT – 19 points

MIDDLE ROW
★ ★ ★

"A"

What is the longest word that can be typed using the middle row keys of a typewriter a maximum of once?

202

RUN FOR IT
★

A race over 50 metres results in Vicky beating her twin sister Kris by 10 metres. They decide to have another race, this time with Vicky starting 10 metres behind the start line.

Assuming they run at the same rate as before, who do you think wins now (if anyone)?

"Here's a good trick" said Andrew, offering Sylvia a pack of cards. "Take a card." Sylvia did so and looked at it for a few seconds. "Now put it back into the pack," said Andrew, and Sylvia obliged, putting the card somewhere in the middle of the pack. Andrew squared the pack up well then shuffled it a few times over.

"Now watch," said Andrew. He held the pack in front of Sylvia and as the fingers from his other hand slid up the sides of the pack the card she had chosen emerged straight from the middle of the pack!

Sylvia applauded. "Great trick," she said, "how do you do it?"
"Obviously very well!" said Andrew, "but I will tell you this – I didn't use any glue and I didn't need to know where any of the cards were in the pack."

Sylvia couldn't work out how Andrew rigged his pack. Can you?

Which of these seven symbols is the odd one out when the other six are correctly paired?

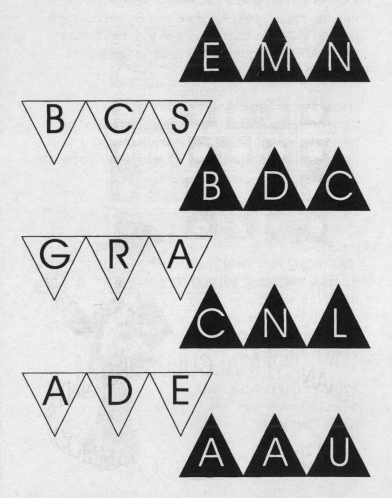

DOMINO DERBY

★ ★ ★ ★ ★

Shade out one dot from every domino so that the numbers of remaining dots in each row, column and both main diagonals are the same.

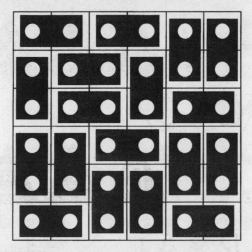

206

LENGTH MATTERS

★

The longest word that can be read here is...?

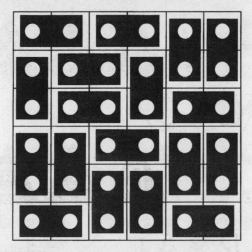

TRUANCYLICALCULUSURPRINTE
COMMANDODECAGONISEAPOR

207 NOT NEXT
★★★★

Place the numbers 1 through 8 in the boxes below so that no two boxes connected by a straight black line contain consecutive numbers.

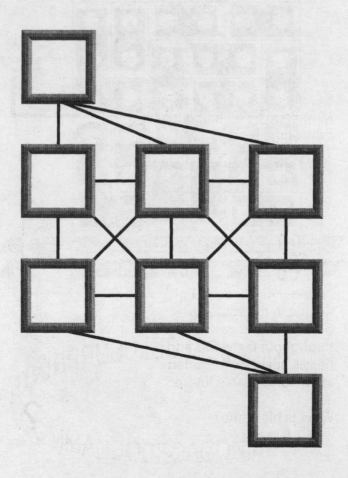

208 GET UP STEAM
★ ★

Professor Muddleup wants to make a refreshing, hot cup of coffee. However, he wants it to remain hot for as long as possible so he wishes to boil his water as long as possible.

Professor Reader (that's you) comes along and sees Muddleup's kettle boiling away. "Just leave that for a few more moments please, I like my coffee really hot," says Muddleup as he munches his break-time biscuits.

What should you point out to him?

209 FAME PILLS?
★ ★ ★ ★ ★

A man takes a couple of tablets. As a result, he becomes famous throughout the world and he will never be forgotten in the foreseeable future.

What is his name?

Spell out an eleven letter word, travelling along each line once only.

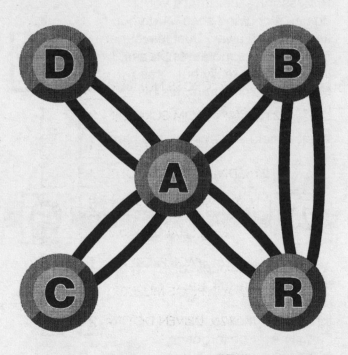

Time Limit – 90 minutes

For each correctly solved puzzle award yourself the number of points shown in the table below. See if you can beat the target.

	VALUE	SCORE
211. STEP ON UP	2	
212. CROSS NUMBER	5	
213. START FROM SCRATCH	3	
214. CHIRAL BIAS	1	
215. DIVIDE & CONQUER	4	
216. SWORD WORDS	5	
217. SHAPELY SUM	3	
218. SPACE PROJECT	1	
219. A TYPE OF MURDER	4	
220. DRIVEN DOTTY	2	
TOTAL (max. 30)		

TARGET TO BEAT – 20 points

Complete this crossword to find the unclued word at 10 Across.

ACROSS

2 Si, señor (3)
4 Cloth has a sleep (3)
6 It tends to mar reputations (4)
8 Artists use it, if burnt (5)
10 YOUR ANSWER (6)
12 Your relation from France? (5)
13 Made of soap or flour (4)
14 Cut (3)
15 Born, sounding like a horse? (3)

DOWN

1 Governmental survey (6)
3 Type of fishy pink? (6)
5 The people (6)
7 Make known (6)
9 Believe, calculate (6)
11 Get less shallow (6)

212 CROSS NUMBER
★ ★ ★ ★ ★

Place nine different digits into the spaces so that six correct equations are formed simultaneously.

213 START FROM SCRATCH
★ ★ ★

The tiles below are each scratched by the three rods on the right. How many of the nine possible scratches will there be on the tiles, in total?

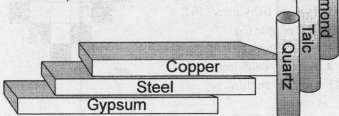

173

CHEIROL BIAS

★

On which side of the line would you place Italy in order to preserve the hidden logic?

Cyprus ┆ Gibraltar
Japan ┆ Argentina
India ┆ U.S.A.
United Kingdom ┆ Denmark

 DIVIDE & CONQUER

★ ★ ★

Divide this square into sections by drawing two straight lines (which cross at some point in the square) so that the sum of the digits in each section is the same.

$$6$$
$$5 \quad 2$$
$$3 \quad 8$$
$$1$$
$$7$$

Sword Words are words which form an anagram of another word, such as ARTISTE and TASTIER. Each clue suggests a pair of Sword Words. For each pair, ONE of the two words will fit into the grid below.

When completed, the letters in the arrowed column can themselves be rearranged to make two six-letter Sword Words. What are they?

⬇

1) What the Speaking Clock does?
☐ M ☐ T

2) Cosy African antelopes
S ☐ U ☐

3) Two fruits
L ☐ ☐ ☐ N

4) Norwegian Spanish man
S ☐ ☐ O ☐

5) Used even more disgraceful language
☐ ☐ O ☐ E

6) Irregular bullfighters on horseback
☐ ☐ ☐ R ☐ ☐ I ☐

Clue for final Sword Words :
Crib for a Berlin baby?

☐ ☐ ☐ ☐ ☐ ☐
☐ ☐ ☐ ☐ ☐ ☐

175

217 SHAPELY SUM
★ ★ ★

Which shape (A, B or C) fits into the grid on the left to make it mathematically correct?

11	2		7	
				5
5				
	7			12
4		13		3

11	4
	3	12
	1

A

6	7
	2	23
	4

B

14	8
	4	2
		5

C

218 SPACE PROJECT
★

In a national competition children were invited to design experiments to put aboard the next Space Shuttle flight. This attracted much attention in the Science class at Southbury School. One pupil was interested in animal psychology. In particular, she suggested an experiment to observe how birds would respond to weightlessness, by seeing whether they would attempt to fly in their cage.

"I don't think NASA would think much of having dead birds on board!" her teacher said. The pupil could not understand why the teacher was so damning of her experiment – she had made sure in designing it that there would be enough air, water and food for the birds to survive. Can you spot the child's mistake?

The detective entered the room and turned the light on. Jack Steel was found dead, slumped over his computer keyboard. "Looks like Jack's been working too hard for his poor old heart," said the detective. His assistant took a closer look at the screen :

```
qnd so I hqve
decided to tqke my
life. Pleqse tell my
zife thqt I love her
deqrly but I hope
she understqnds my
reqsons. There qre
too mqny auestions.
```

The assistant beckoned to his superior. "This seems curious for a suicide. Obviously the garbage at the bottom is what he typed when he collapsed on this standard keyboard, but what about the rest?"

"Take a printout," said the detective. "With this evidence we can cut down our enquiries substantially."

What sort of suspects should they look for?

Remember how to do dot-to-dot? Trace a path from letter to letter (you will notice that we've already joined up the first word, WHAT). Then tell us what the answer to the riddle is.

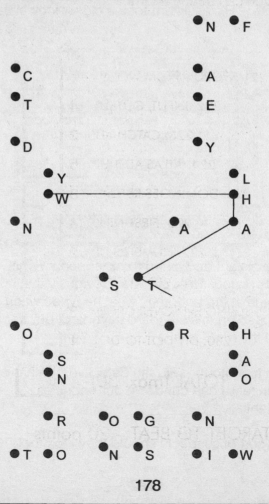

LAP 23

Time Limit – **90 minutes**

For each correctly solved puzzle award yourself
the number of points shown in the table below.
See if you can beat the target.

	VALUE	SCORE
221. WORDS FROM WORDS	1	
222. INPUT, OUTPUT	4	
223. CATCH ALL	2	
224. ATLAS ADD-UP	5	
225. DOMINOES RETURN	3	
226. FIRST NINE	4	
227. NUMBERS UP	2	
228. WORD CUBE	5	
229. SEEING RED OVER GREEN	3	
230. DIY DOT-TO-DOT	1	
TOTAL (max. 30)		

TARGET TO BEAT – 20 points

★

Use the letters of PUZZLE TWO HUNDRED AND TWENTY-ONE once each to form five words. Clues and some letters to start you off are provided.

Clue						
Unit of power			T			
Made into regions	Z				D	
Underground passage		U				L
Gentle breeze				H		R
Badly hurt	W		U			

---

222   INPUT, OUTPUT   

★ ★ ★ ★

Several different numbers are put into a computer program which uses a simple formula to determine the number it outputs. Can you tell us what formula the computer is using?

$$1 \rightarrow -1$$
$$2 \rightarrow 0$$
$$4 \rightarrow 8$$
$$6 \rightarrow 24$$
$$10 \rightarrow 80$$

In the three pictures below, a rope is loosely wound around a central pole. When the ends of the rope are pulled away in the direction shown, which picture represents a situation where the rope will catch on the pole?

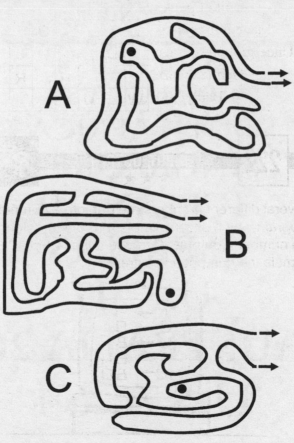

A

B

C

Can you work out the reasoning behind the numbers and thus provide us with the number for Canada?

LIBYA 1
JAPAN 2
FRANCE 3
MAURITIUS 4
JAMAICA 5
SOUTH AFRICA 7
SINGAPORE 8
ICELAND 9
ISRAEL 13
U.K. 17
AUSTRALIA 20
U.S.A. 64

Place the dominoes in the grid in order to form a total of ten English words across and down.

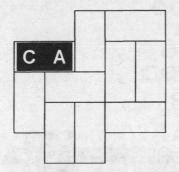

I boast that if I take seven of the nine letters below, I can make an English word from them. Can you?

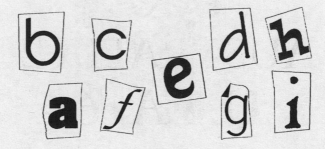

NUMBERS UP
★ ★

What is the last number in this sequence and why?

100
500
1
50
1000
5
?

228

WORD CUBE
★ ★ ★ ★ ★

Make up to three twists on this puzzle cube so that it is possible to read two six-letter words.
Hint – Don't worry about the orientation of the letters, and the number 9 is a clue.

A man stands in the middle of a busy market square on a hot, sunny day. The man takes out a rectangular piece of white cloth from a basket and sets light to it. A few passers-by wonder why he is doing this, but seem unconcerned.

The man then takes out a piece of blue cloth and does the same thing. Again, no one pays very much attention. The man repeats this feat a further six times with red, yellow, black, purple, orange and pink cloths.

Finally, the man takes out a plain green piece of cloth. When he sets it alight, a crowd of distressed onlookers quickly gathers and before long the local police arrive on the scene to arrest him. The man was sentenced in court to a very long jail sentence.

Why did the man get arrested?

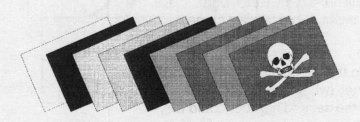

Each of the curves in the lower diagram can be placed between a pair of black dots in the upper diagram. Do this for all the lines so that a simple picture is formed.

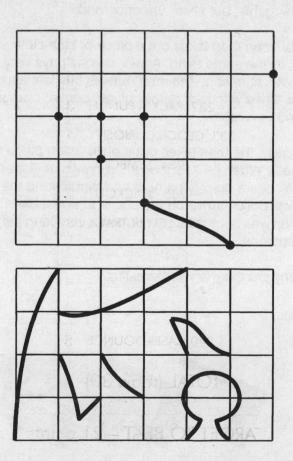

Time Limit – 90 minutes

For each correctly solved puzzle award yourself the number of points shown in the table below. See if you can beat the target.

	VALUE	SCORE
231. MINI CROSS	5	
232. PACK A PUNCH	3	
233. CLOCK CURIOSITY	1	
234. SYMBOLIC	4	
235. BLACKOUT	2	
236. LETTER TRACK	3	
237. GROOVY	1	
238. CUBE VIEW	4	
239. POLISH CODE?	2	
240. LASER BOUNCE	5	
TOTAL (max. 30)		

TARGET TO BEAT – 21 points

Solve the miniature cryptic crossword, then rearrange the shaded letters to form your seven-letter answer.

ACROSS
1 Branch backs New York baseball team (4)
5 Seasonal variation which turns (4)
6 Green plant in seasonal garden (4)
7 Donna used on the oboe (4)

DOWN
1 Celebrity makes rodents turn back (4)
2 Tesselate slab (4)
3 Advantage at the boundary (4)
4 Lady upset alcoholic drink (4)

232 PACK A PUNCH ★★★

In which order would you put these cards on top of one another to form a correct multiplication sum?

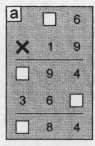

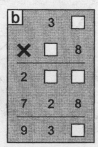

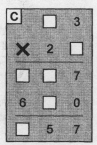

Professor Muddleup was considering an interesting question. He has a large number of modern and antique clocks around the walls of his laboratory. Of these, quite a number of the modern ones do not have numerals on them.

"If that's the case," he wondered, "how am I to know which way up the clock should go? Some of these clocks don't have any marks or other indications that show the user where 12 o'clock is supposed to be."

Tell the Professor why you should never see upside-down clocks, even on models with completely blank faces. (The answer has nothing to do with manufacturer markings on the back of the clock.)

SYMBOLIC
★ ★ ★ ★

Replace every circle with a number (the same for each circle). Repeat this process with the diamond, and again with the triangle, so that in all you have only used three different numbers. If you have solved the puzzle correctly, the seven rows, columns and diagonal will each add up to the totals indicated.

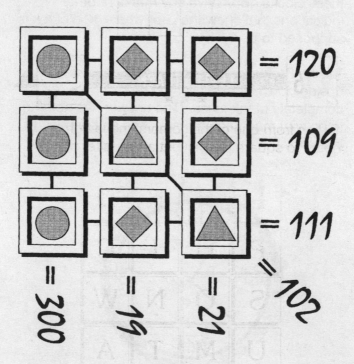

= 120

= 109

= 111

= 300

= 19

= 21

= 102

190

235 BLACKOUT ★★

Shade out eight squares to form four congruent areas (that is, identical in shape and size).

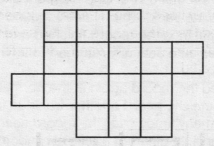

236 LETTER TRACK ★★★

Starting from one of the corners, move from square to square to spell out an 11-letter word.

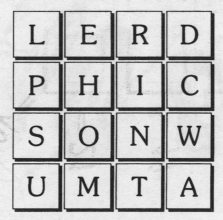

L	E	R	D
P	H	I	C
S	O	N	W
U	M	T	A

Madeleine was playing her long-playing record collection the other day when she came across one of her brother's LPs. She played it and listened to the track, which lasted around four minutes. But then the record finished and the pick-up arm was automatically returned to its holder.

She started the record again in the normal fashion and this time she heard another track! In fact, after playing it many times over the record seemed to play about eight different tracks at random.

How was this possible?

CUBE VIEW
★ ★ ★ ★

Which two pieces, when welded together, will form a complete 3 x 3 x 3 cube?

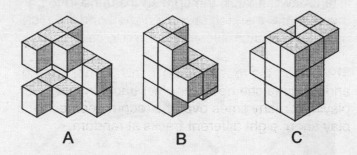

A   B   C

POLISH CODE?
★ ★

This is a message coded using one of the oldest cryptographic methods known to man. Can you read what it says?

What is the LEAST number of double-sided mirrors that must be rotated through 90 degrees in order to direct the laser beam to hit the sensor? The blocks will absorb the light so these need to be avoided.

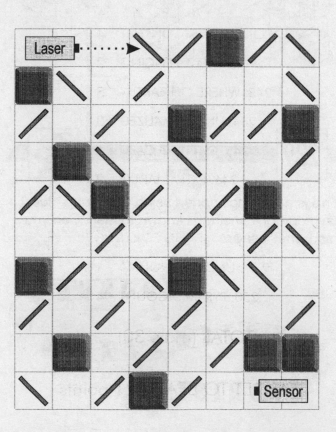

LAP 25

Time Limit – 90 minutes

For each correctly solved puzzle award yourself
the number of points shown in the table below.
See if you can beat the target.

	VALUE	SCORE
241. CONSONANT CONTENT	4	
242. FENCING	2	
243. WHERE ON EARTH?	5	
244. UNDECIMALIZED	3	
245. CUTTING CARD	1	
246. EXTRA! !ARTXE	2	
247. FIND THEM	5	
248. SPRING FOR IT	3	
249. ROUND AND ROUND	1	
250. PYRAMID COUNT	4	

TOTAL (max. 30)

TARGET TO BEAT – 21 points

241 — CONSONANT CONTENT
★ ★ ★ ★

"A"

Put the consonants back into this mini-crossword. The brackets show you the rows from where half of the letters came.

CSX??? {

CLMV???? {

CNY??? {

242 — FENCING
★ ★

I have some fence posts which I want to use in my garden. Each post is four feet high and between the tops of each pair of posts there hangs a chain.

Each section of chain is six feet long. How close does each pair of fence posts needs to be so that the chain hangs exactly one foot from the ground at its lowest point?

Have you heard this one? "An explorer travels 10 miles south, 10 miles east, then 10 miles north and ends back where he started. Where is his base camp?"

Of course you have, the answer is the North Pole. However, we're not going to ask you the obvious question.

Many puzzle-lovers get the answer to this question partly wrong, or at least, not entirely correct. Although the North Pole is correct, there is also another answer. In fact, an infinite number of answers. We want to know, "Where does there exist an infinite number of points that also satisfy the requirements of this puzzle?"

(In fact, if you think hard enough, there are many, many different answers!)

244 UNDECIMALIZED
★ ★ ★

In Britain, pounds, shillings and pence were decimalized into our current £s and new pence in 1971. In France, the National Assembly decided upon the metric system of measurement (using decimal figures) in 1791.

However, there was one occasion when there used to be 10 of something which were then "undecimalized" to a larger number, all because of two people. Can you think of the occasion I am referring to?

245 CUTTING CARD
★

A quickie – how many squares of 3 x 3 inches (below left) can be cut from the large 22 x 18 inch piece of card (below right)?

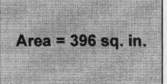

Area = 9 sq. in.

Area = 396 sq. in.

Sharon had received a telegram from the Queen to congratulate her on reaching her 100th birthday. Sharon's sisters, Marjorie and Norah, are seen in the front-page photo of the local newspaper looking at the telegram.

The next day, Sharon noticed something unusual about the headline. Can you spot it?

THE DARLINGTON DAILY

MARGE LETS NORAH SEE SHARON'S TELEGRAM!

247 FIND THEM
★ ★ ★ ★ ★

Find two DIFFERENT integers that satisfy the following property :

"Take the first number, square it, then subtract the number itself. This gives us a result (let's call it A). Now take the second number and do exactly the same thing, to give us result B. We require A and B to be the same."

Now : list (so far as is possible) EVERY pair of numbers that satisfies this property.

248 SPRING FOR IT
★ ★ ★

The left-hand diagrams show how one spring behaves, measured against a ruler. What will be the total distance (marked) AFTER the weight is attached in the right-hand diagram?

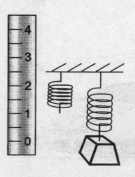

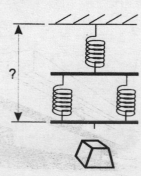

200

A large group of people board a train. They do so with the full knowledge that they are going to end up at the same place from which they started, and there are no stops along the way. The passengers aren't going to see any rolling landscapes or any local areas of interest.

The passengers have paid money for the trip, but the managers of the train have had very few complaints about the route covered. The train has been running for a number of months but is due to close down soon. It will re-open in the same location next year to follow an identical route.

The train operates many times a day, taking different groups of people each time although a few people sometimes take the journey more than once in the same day.

What sort of train is this?

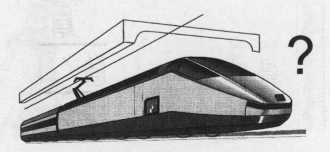

If you added the number of edges this pyramid-based figure has to the number of faces it has, the total you would get is...?

TOP
SECRET

1. Across : Satin, Meats, Assay; Down : Samba, Teams, Nasty.

2. 3 pence. Multiples of 2p coins account for even numbered values. One 5p coin and multiples of 2p account for 5p, 7p, 9p, 11p etc. Hence all values above 3p are accounted for.

3. Place the weights as follows:

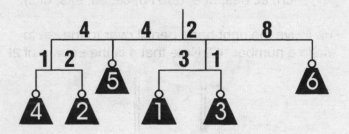

Moment on L.H.S. = ((4 + 2) x 8) + (5 x 4) = 68
Moment on R.H.S. = ((1 + 3) x 2) + (6 x 10) = 68
Hence balances.

4. From back to front, the letters spell out CHEIROMANCY (the art of reading palms).

5. They all have eyes.

6. They do not rhyme with any other words in the English language.

7. 105, since it is the sum 1 + 2 + 3 + ... + 14.

8. Around 34m. The projectile spends much more time in the upper half of the flight path because the vertical acceleration reduces to zero before the ball starts falling downward.

9. Between H and B. They are ordered alphabetically according to their phonetic sound (ay, aitch, ar, bee, dee, dub'l u, ee, eff, eks, etc.).

10. Move the right-hand pencil over to the left to make a number "4". Note that 4 is the square of 2!

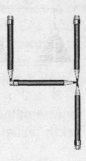

11. Bishop (as in chess), Putter, Domino.

12. 22 years, since $1 + 2 + 3 + ... + 22 = 253$.

13. 35 turns to spell WARY. When the largest cog turns one revolution, the other cogs turn a distance of 143 teeth also. The R cog will be upright every 143 teeth, likewise for the A cog every 35 teeth. The M cog displays a letter (M or W) every 11 teeth. The Y cog looks the same every 13 teeth for a similar reason. But "every 11" and "every 13" occurs as a consequence of turning the R cog 143 teeth (since 11 times 13 equals 143). So we need only concern ourselves with the R and the A cogs. Since 35 and 143 are co-prime (that is, they have no common factors: $35 = 7 \times 5$, $143 = 11 \times 13$) then we require 35 turns of the large R cog before the A cog is also in the right place.

14. F, because they represent the places First, Second, Third and Fourth (initial letters).

15. Picture 3; the others are all the same up to rotation. Picture 3 is a reflection of the other pictures.

16. HIJACKER. All the words in the box contain three consecutive letters of the alphabet (eg. eCDEmite, moNOPoly, etc.).

17. 400,065 wires. If there were, say, ten cities, we would need ten more wires to add an eleventh city. Likewise a twelfth city would need eleven more wires, and so on. So the answer we need is the answer to the sum 1 + 2 + ... + 893 + 894. Notice that this is equal to 447 pairs of 895 (look at the first and last number, then the second first and second last number etc. – all these pairs add up to 895). So the answer is 447 x 895 = 400,065.

18. Pocket 2. Remember that the angle the ball makes with the cushion would be identical before and after the rebound.

19. Experiment 1, because water at 20 degrees Fahrenheit is ice!

20. A grey G on a white background.
The code used is :
Background colour – white if the letter has no holes in it (like 'M'), grey if it has one (like 'D'), black if it has two (like '8'); Foreground colour – black if the letter is made up of purely straight lines, white if made purely out of curved lines, grey if it is a mixture of straight and curved lines.

21. On the rope – Repaid, Diaper; On the chain – Serif, Fires. Use the E and the I in the intersections.

22. 8, because

> the difference between 2 and 6 is 4
> the difference between 2 and 3 is 1
> the difference between 6 and 3 is 3

The total of these differences is 4 + 1 + 3 = 8. The same rule applies to all the triangles.

23. Short-sightedness. It is a diverging lens that helps push light rays apart and therefore corrects the over-strong eyeball lens that short-sighted people have.

24. This mystery relies on the fact that calculator and telephone keypads have different layouts, so when I pressed the same pattern of keys on the telephone the numbers were wrong except for the middle row (4, 5, 6).

1	2	3
4	5	6
7	8	9

0 Telephone

7	8	9
4	5	6
1	2	3

Calculator 0

25. Ten routes.

26. Removing the first letter from each word gives : "How his old russian hat raises laughter, laughter rings out".

27. 45 seconds. A will have swung 5 times, B will have swung 3.

28. All geostationary satellites have to circle around the Earth's equator so that the centripetal acceleration counteracts the radial acceleration. Also, these satellites have to be at a specific height. Therefore there is only really one narrow band of orbits these satellites can take.

29. A glove.

30. The "E" pin. Incidentally, did you notice the pins spell the word BACKFIELD when picked up in order?

31. Enlist, tinsel, listen, Silent.

32. 15, 12, 14, 13, 11 respectively. The numbers are consecutive and add up to 65 so must be 11 to 15 in some order. Using this together with the 1st and 3rd equations (the ones relating to the triangle and square) tells you the number in the circle must be 14. Using the 1st and 4th equation tells you the numbers at the ends add up to 26. Using the first equation we find the number in the square is one less than the second number. Equation 3 says the last two numbers add up to 24, so the first number is two larger than the fourth.

33. By Newton's Third Law of Motion : "Every action has an equal and opposite reaction". In the same way that you feel "heavier" when in a lift going upwards, when a ring is thrown it actually "weighs" more than 10kg's worth of force and the bridge could then give way.

34. NEEDY, because if five lines are added to the words on the left we get SOAR = RISE, FLAX = CLOTH, CHAR = BURN, MANX = CAT and POOR = NEEDY.

35. The black and white letters, when read in a zigzag pattern give : Mountain-top and Postulation in the top grid, and Contraption and Labradorean in the bottom grid.

36. FIGURATIVE. F-Clef, I-Spy, G-String, U-Boat, A-Bomb, T-Junction, V-Neck are well known. "R-months" are when one is not supposed to eat oysters. An I-Beam is a girder. The E-Layer is part of the atmosphere from which long-range radio waves are reflected.

37. Either 75 or 95, depending on the design of the cards. Each card has either two or four diamonds in the corners which have to be included as well as the main pips.

38. Measure the diameter of the bottom of the bottle. Half it, square it, and multiply by pi to get the surface area of the bottom of the bottle. Measure the height of the liquid and add it to the height of the air when the bottle is turned upside down. Multiply the total with the previously obtained surface area to get the volume of the bottle.

39. Paper aircraft! However, according to the *Guinness Book of Records*, a distance of 1.25 miles has been recorded by throwing a paper airplane from the top floor of a tall building.

40. Five balls, since there are 10 balls present and visual inspection confirms this must be a 15-ball triangle. No estimation is necessary.

41. UNITER, because it only has three vowels whereas all the other words have four.

42. 0%. For all such numbers, the sum of the digits is $1 + 2 + 3 + ... + 9 = 45$, which is 5 x 9. This means that the sum of the digits is divisible by 9, and hence (by a well-known mathematical rule) the number itself is divisible by 9. Therefore none of the numbers are prime.

43. Twice as fast. The idlers can be ignored. Since A has twice the number of teeth as J it must be going half as fast.

44. In Scandinavian countries the date is written in the International Date format of YY/MM/DD, so the spy should have put 46/10/12 as his date of birth in order not to arouse suspicion.

45. Picture 1, since the letters A, B, C, D, E, F have been put behind a window.

46. There are 38 words you could use. The most common are bejewel, beveled, beveler, jeweler, jezebel, levered, leverer, leveret, nemeses, receder, redefer, referee, relevel, renewer, reveler, revered, reverer, severer, sewered, venerer.

47. 132, since :

$$1 \times 2 = 2$$
$$3 \times 4 = 12$$
$$5 \times 6 = 30$$
$$7 \times 8 = 56$$
$$9 \times 10 = 90$$
$$11 \times 12 = 132.$$

48. You should check that your friend hasn't boiled his egg, which would make the egg spin for far longer.

49. The answer is FOUR. To see why, suppose the answer was SEVEN. This cannot be correct because this answer has 5 letters, not 7. However, FOUR does have 4 letters and is a valid answer. In fact it is the only number, when spelled out in letters, that has the same amount of letters as the number specifies.

50. SEMESTER.

51. Anything that could be prefixed by "Seventh", so Heaven and Day are acceptable answers. The series goes First Aid, Second Guess, Third Degree, Fourth Estate, etc.

52. One answer is :

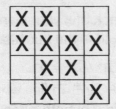

53. Bar magnets are active only at their ends, but act just like ordinary iron bars in the middle. Here, if bar 1 sticks to bar 2 then 2 is a magnet, and vice versa if bars 1 and 2 swap positions.

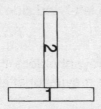

54. UNDERGROUND and ANTIOXIDANT. Notice some letters are used twice.

55. The letters of MONOCHROME are seen.

56. PASTER (the clues give Master, Poster, Patter, Passer, Pastor, Pastes).

57. No. Pythagoras' Theorem says that for a right-angled triangle :

$$x^2 + y^2 = z^2$$

where z is the length of the side opposite the right-angle. For the triangle in the question this means :

$$a^2 + a^2 = b^2$$
$$2a^2 = b^2$$

Taking the square root of both sides :

$$\sqrt{2}a = b$$

Therefore a and b can never both be whole numbers, since the left-hand side is now an irrational number.

58. (a). Like any buoyant object, the balloon will want to oppose the gravitational field ("g-force") felt by the car.

59. The "Eagle" lunar spaceship module which lies in the Sea of Tranquillity on the Moon.

60. The picture of the guitar is incorrect as one of its six strings is missing.

215

61. They are all words that can be spelt phonetically using one letter : the pictures are a Bee (B), Pea (P), Ewe (U), Jay (J), Tea (T), Eye (I).

62. Father lent them another pound coin so that they had 24 coins. Thus Albert gets £12, Bernard gets £8, Claire gets £3. This leaves one coin left over, which they give back.

63. The probability of a head followed by a tail is equal to that of a tail followed by a head, despite the bias. Therefore toss the coin twice and keep doing so until you get a pair of tosses which are dissimilar. Take the first result of these tosses.

64. Most parachutes NEED a hole in them! If they didn't let some air through, the parachute would swing wildly from side to side.

65. The picture of the dice. This picture shows the 3 and 4 dot sides in the wrong places – they add up to 7 and therefore should be opposite one another.

66. They all make five new words when read backwards – Lamina, Diaper, Reward, Spacer and Snoops.

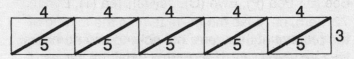

67. 25 feet. If you imagine unravelling the column you would find it looks like :

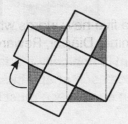

Since 3 squared plus 4 squared equals 5 squared (by Pythagoras' Theorem), and as there are five complete spirals around the column, the answer is $5 \times 5 = 25$.

68. I am most probably blocking the small hole drilled into the casing of the pen, preventing the pressure from equalizing. Therefore no ink comes out.

69. The items above the line require colour to distinguish between the identical parts.

70. 20 square centimetres. Since the figure can be rearranged into five squares, and since there were four squares to start with, each new square must be 0.8 of an old square. We use $0.8 \times 25 = 20$.

71. MATHEMATICAL. The clues refer to mat-he-ma-ti-cal and lac-it-am-eh-tam.

72. Zero, because the (n–n) term in the middle of the product equals zero; multiplying any numbers by zero equals zero, no matter what the values of the numbers are.

73. Both directions (rocking back and forth, first anticlockwise then clockwise).

74. Suitable answers include : (i) Square manholes can only fit in the hole four ways. Round holes fit any way. (ii) They can be rolled into position. (iii) They use less material than a square manhole of equal width. (iv) They cannot possibly fall through the hole (square manholes can fall through the diagonal). (v) They have no sharp corners.

75. The answer is :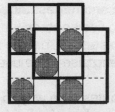

Since the diagram is basically made up of 15 squares, and since each shape has to have one of the five dots, then each piece must be made up of

3 squares. These must either be L-shapes (as shown) or 3-square rods (which doesn't work).

76. W. The letters within the circle, trapezium, triangle and square make up the words Spring, Winter, Summer and Autumn respectively.

77. Xavier, Yves and Zillah should all buy Wilf a drink. This is because Wilf owes one drink but is owed four drinks. Xavier owes two drinks and is owed one drink, so owes a drink. Likewise, Yves and Zillah owe one drink. This gives the answer.

78. Only statement 5 is correct. 1 and 2 are clearly wrong, otherwise pulleys would be pointless. There would be less friction in system A because there are less rubbing surfaces, so A is more energy efficient. Hence 5 is right and 3 is wrong. 4 is incorrect because A requires more force to be applied over a shorter distance.

79. All the items above the line have to be put inside something else to be useful.

80. Thirteen routes. The way to work it out is to calculate the number of ways to arrive at each junction in turn.

81. (one) NIGHT STAND, (two) TIMING, (three) WISE MEN, (four) POSTER BED, (five) SENSES, (six) PACK, (seven) SEAS, (eight) DAY CLOCK, (nine) LIVES, (ten) COMMANDMENTS.

82. $23. Suppose we consider all the possible bets as follows:

$5 chips only cover 0, 5, 10, 15, 20, 25, 30, 35, 40, ...
One $7 chip + $5 chips cover 7, 12, 17, 22, 27, ...
Two $7 chips + $5 chips cover 14, 19, 24, 29, 34, ...
Three $7 chips + $5 chips cover 21, 26, 31, 36, 41, ...
Four $7 chips + $5 chips cover 28, 33, 38, 43, 48, ...
Five $7 chips + $5 chips cover 35, 40, ... again.

So each series covers all the numbers ending in 0/5, 7/2, 4/9, 1/6 or 3/8. But the 3/8 series begins at 28 onwards, so 3, 8, 13, 18, and 23 can't be made. 23 is the largest of these.

83. Only one. By placing two feet on the same level (which can always be done) the third foot is then adjusted until the camera becomes level.

84. YES, because you take the last letters of the acronyms. So VSO is voluntarY servicE overseaS, hence Y, E, S. The other acronyms are AfricaN NationaL CongresS (taking last letters gives NLS), extrA sensorY perceptioN (AYN), highesT commoN factoR (TNR), and inteR continentaL ballistiC missilE (RLCE).

85. STATEN ISLAND, New York Harbor. Read the arrows in order as if they were the minute hand of a clock at five-minute intervals.

86. Meltdown, signpost, foxglove, offspring, weekday.

87. 4/3, or four thirds. You can work it out by :

$$4a = a + 4$$
$$3a = 4$$

Dividing both sides by 3 :

$$a = \tfrac{4}{3}$$

88. After 504 seconds, which is the lowest common multiple of 6, 7, 8 and 9.

89. The man could have stabbed himself with an icicle.

90. Pages 16, 25 and 26. Page 16 must be missing because it is on the back of page 15. The supplement must be numbered from 13 to 28, so the sum of the pages on each leaf must add up to $(13 + 14 + 27 + 28 =)$ 82. Likewise 15 + 16 + 25 + 26 = 82.

91. A in a diamond. Reading downwards row-by-row, the like symbols spell out the names of five countries : Egypt, Italy, Kenya, Libya, Yemen.

92. Luckily for Postie Pete, the hole was a catflap measuring 20 by 21 centimetres. The letter can easily be slotted through the diagonal which is 29 cms long :

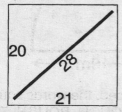

93. (ii), since we use the formula for the area of a circle :

$$Area = \pi \times (radius)^2$$
$$Area\ of\ black\ tyre = (\pi \times 5^2) - (\pi \times 4^2)$$
$$= (25 - 16)\pi = 9\pi$$
$$= \pi \times 3^2 = Area\ of\ inner\ hub$$

94. Everyone jumped in to have a swim but forgot to put a ladder out so that they could get back on the boat.

95. 10 metres also. Imagine the ladder was in the opposite direction. It is a radius of the circle whose radius we know to be 10 metres.

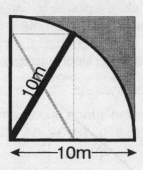

96. When pronounced, the words sound like other words : BOUGH, DOUGH, ROUGH, THROUGH, each of which ends in OUGH.

97. He is probably a shopkeeper or other merchant. 12 + 25% = 16 is correct because it means 12 + (25% of 16) = 16. The 25% addition represents the profit margin on the 12 he wishes to add. If £15 was the selling price, the extra £3 would only give a 20% profit.

98. None – only petrol engines use spark plugs.

99. Add a line to the top of the 10 to give :
        20 TO 5 = 4.40.

100. The Statue of Liberty is back-to-front.

101. Blurb, Fluff, Going, Nylon, Plump (also Pin-up, Polyp, Pop-up, Primp), Widow.

102. 48 points. It takes 4 points to win a game, so to win 2 sets requires 2 x 6 x 4 = 48.

103. Picture 5 cannot be folded up to make a cube.

104. 210, because the series is comprised of the powers of two (1, 2, 4, 8, 16, 32, 64, 128, 256, etc.) grouped into threes.

105. Simply change the corner lines.

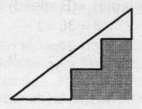

The area of the original triangle was 0.5 x 4 x 3 = 6. Taking away the three shaded squares leaves an area of 3 squares.

106. They are the longest words that can be made using only consonants.

107. 50 feet in diameter, because :

$$r^2 = x^2 + y^2 \text{ for a circle}$$
$$r^2 = (r-5)^2 + (r-10)^2$$
$$0 = r^2 - 30r + 125$$
$$r = \frac{30 \pm \sqrt{900 - 500}}{2} \text{ using the formula for a quadratic equation}$$
$$= \frac{30 \pm 20}{2} = 25 \text{ or } 5$$

It can't be 5 since that's too small, so it must be 25 feet in radius; i.e. 50 feet in diameter.

108. 6 revolutions per minute.

$$(\text{A speed}) \times (\text{A teeth}) = (\text{B speed}) \times (\text{B teeth})$$
$$27 \times 8 = 36 \times ?$$
$$? = \frac{27 \times 8}{36} = 6$$

109. Between the 7 and the 2. The order depends on the number of "segments" required to make up the digital number. 7 uses three segments, 2 uses five, and 4 uses four.

110. c3, c5, c7, e3, e7, g3, g5. Adding the knights here protects the (as yet undefended) squares h1, g2, a8, b1, a2, b3, h7, g8 and f7.

111. Skyjack, Buzzsaw, Grapevine, Rendezvous, Headquarters.

112. 51, because $3 + 5 + 7 = 15$, digits reversed $= 51$.

113. He was on a rotating space ship. The coin refuses to spin because it has inertia (and therefore is trying to counteract the gravitational forces on it) but the opposition force is changing all the time because it is on an already spinning space ship.

114. Either E (for zero point fivE) or F (for halF) are correct answers. Likewise, eleveN $= 11$, hundreD $= 100$, siX $= 6$, twentY $= 20$.

115. It is the Arc de Triomphe in Paris.

116. PUMP, to give Bicycle Pump, Beer Pump, Hand Pump, Water Pump.

117. 17160. There are fifteen possible places to put the black. From the remaining fourteen spaces suppose we number the yellow balls 1 to 7. There are fourteen places to put ball 1, thirteen to put ball 2, and so on until ball 7 is put in any of eight places. Therefore this gives

$$14 \times 13 \times 12 \times 11 \times 10 \times 9 \times 8 = 17,297,280$$

However, the yellow balls all look the same. There are:

$$7 \times 6 \times 5 \times 4 \times 3 \times 2 \times 1 = 5,040$$

different ways of numbering the balls. (The red balls are already accounted for since they take up the remaining spaces.) Remembering we have to divide by three (since the triangle can be rotated 120 degrees) the answer is :

$$\left(15 \times \frac{14 \times 13 \times 12 \times 11 \times 10 \times 9 \times 8}{7 \times 6 \times 5 \times 4 \times 3 \times 2 \times 1}\right) \div 3 = 17,160$$

118. (b). Both ends are raised, but (because of the different radii of the rotating cylinders) the left-hand side winds up faster than the right-hand side.

119. Sundials always go "clockwise" because of the Earth's rotation around the Sun. Early civilizations used sundials as their first timing devices.

120. 3. The number in each shape represents the number of neighbours the shape has.

121. They are all palindromes (i.e. the words read the same backwards and forwards). The pictures represent Noon, Rotor, Eye, Sexes, Kayak, Radar.

122. £64.78 is not divisible by four, whereas all the components of the total (2780, 32, 88, 12) are.

123. One face and one edge.

124. Atom, Atop and Stow (A to M, A to P, S to W).

125. Add a leaf to squares c1 and e5, a star to a3 and d4, and a circle to b2 and a4.

126. They make up "portmanteau words" :
Breakfast + Lunch = Brunch
Chuckle + Snort = Chortle
Flame + Glare = Flare
Glamorous + Ritz = Glitz
Motor + Hotel = Motel
Smoke + Fog = Smog

127. 951. Each number in the series is found by adding the previous three numbers, so the last figure is 153 + 281 + 517 = 951.

128. Die 3, because the "B" face should be the other way up.

129. A whip. The end of the whip can travel at speeds of up to 700 miles per hour. The "cracking" sound is in fact a miniature sonic boom.

130. The answers are :

The diagrams are the results of two dice, one with black dots, one with white dots, merged together.

131. T, since the letters spell out ROMEO and JULIET alternately.

132. £15,000. If one writes out the information in the form of equations :

$$7 \text{ acres} + \text{profit} = £24,000$$
$$\ominus \ 4 \text{ acres} + \text{profit} = £15,000$$
$$\overline{3 \text{ acres} = £9,000}$$

So 4 acres costs £12,000 and (using the middle equation above) we can see that the profit the estate agent makes is £3,000. We are told this is the same on either deal.

The only way the agent could sell 26 acres is by five deals (three lots of 4 acres, two lots of 7 acres). Making £3,000 on each deal means the total profit is £15,000.

133. CONGENIAL. The chemical symbols for the elements are Co, N, Ge, Ni and Al.

134. Move one line from the equals to the minus (effectively changing the positions of the equals and minus signs). Then turn the book upside down! The equation then reads 569 − 288 = 281, a correct sum.

135. An ellipse/oval shape, as shown here :

136. ANTENNA. Removing the first and last two letters of each word gives the numbers ONE, TWO, EIGHT and NINE.

137. 379. For each box, the number is the total of the boxes to the top, top-left and left.

138. 286 per day. There are twelve reversible times for each hour, except that two has to be subtracted for both AM and PM to stop 12:00 being counted twice. So the answer is :

$$((12 \times 12) - 1) \times 2 = 286$$

139. None – steel is less dense than mercury so the balls will float!

140. The lifeboat. All the other objects have holes, you would hope the lifeboat does not!

141. RESTATE. The other words are Estate, State, Tate, Ate.

142. 27 million. If you think of a six figure mileometer (starting with 000001, 000002, etc.) then in any of the six positions the numbers 0 to 9 appear 100,000 times. Hence :
(1+2+3+4+5+6+7+8+9+0) x 100,000 = 4,500,000. Multiplying this by six (for the six digit positions) gives the answer.

143. (c), since copper expands more than platinum, and brass expands more than iron.

144. It is so that 6 and 9 are not confused. If the projectionist looked at these digits on the film it would be possible to get the film the wrong way up.

145. 27 cubes.

146. 5. They are the first positive numbers, when spelled out, to contain the letters of the alphabet : one thousAnd, one Billion, one oCtillion, one hunDreD, onE, Four, eiGht, tHree, so fIve comes next.

[Explanatory note – In the UK the first number is "one hundred And one" (whereas Americans say "one hundred one"), the second number could be

232

1,000,000,000,000 (a UK billion, although the US version is becoming more popular) and the UK octillion is different.]

147. (a) is the correct answer. It can be rigorously proved, but here are a couple of ways of justifying the answer:

Method 1 :
$\frac{1}{3} + \frac{2}{3} = 1$
But $\frac{1}{3} = 0.3333...$
and $\frac{2}{3} = 0.6666...$
So $0.3333... + 0.6666... = 1$
Hence $0.9999.... = 1$

Method 2 :
Let $\quad x = 0.9999...$
So $\quad 10x = 9.9999...$
Hence $\quad 9x = 9$
$\quad\quad\quad x = 1$
So $\ 0.9999... = 1$

148. A paper cup, or other shape which has a base that has a smaller diameter than its open rim.

149. (b), to form MIS "take" NLY = MISTAKENLY. Likewise, HOB"by"IST, UNS"add"LED, NON"plus"SED, AIM"less"LY.

150. Piece 1 is left over.

151. ABSOLUTELY. Split the paragraph up into smaller segments, each of which implies a letter :
Midday = Middle of DAY = A
Starting block = 1st letter of BLOCK = B
Last of the Mohicans = Last letter of MOHICANS = S
Second in Command = 2nd letter in COMMAND = O
and so on.

152. 1 hour. If the steaks are numbered 1 to 6, each having sides a and b, then :
10 mins – brown 1a and 2a; 20 mins – brown 1b and 3a
30 mins – brown 2b and 3b; 40 mins – brown 4a and 5a
50 mins – brown 4b and 6a; 60 mins – brown 5b and 6b

153. 26 cubes. The worm's journey will take him to white and black cubes alternately. There are 14 white cubes and only 13 black cubes so, since he starts at a white cube, he MUST miss out one white cube before ending up at the middle black cube.

154. The correct answer would be "No", because Noah took two of every variety of creature onto the ark. Obviously Noah didn't know that some species (such as snails) are hermaphrodites and are perfectly able to reproduce by themselves.

155. Put X on row 3, Y on row 1, and Z on row 3. The letters on row 1 have vertical symmetry only (that is, their left and right halves are reflections of one another). The letters on row 2 have horizontal

symmetry (their top and bottom halves are reflections). Row 3 contains the letters with 180 degree rotational symmetry (turn them upside down and they look the same). The letters on Row 4 have no symmetry at all.

156. It is the SHORTEST English sentence to use all the letters of the alphabet. (There are shorter sentences but they use abbreviations.)

157. $\frac{50}{\pi}$ or about 15.9 metres.
Circumference of a circle = $2\pi \times$ radius
If the height of the poles is h,
and the radius of the Earth is R,
then $2\pi(R + h) - 2\pi R = 100$
So $2\pi h = 100$, hence $h = 100 \div 2\pi \approx 15.9$m.

158. (b), since no cogs will move at all! The middle cog is being forced in both directions at once. (N.B. Zero is an even number.)

159. An athlete during the course of a 10,000m race, since her right leg would be on the outside of the track.

160. RETSINA (a type of Greek wine).

161. DEATHBED, since you can prefix these letters before each word. D-Day, A-Bomb, T-Shirt, H-Bomb, B-Movie are well known. An E-Boat is indeed a type of boat. An E-Number is a code given to certain food additives by the European Union. A D-Ring is a common piece of equipment used in parachuting and rock climbing.

162. Only one in 3. There are six possible combinations of the bullets. Of these, you only win if the bullets are in chambers 2, 3 and 4 or in 4, 5 and 6.

163. 96, because it only occurs between the hours 00–05, 10–15 and 20–23, six times per hour.

164. DAVID. (D=500 in Roman numerals, V=5, A=first letter, 1=first number).

165. Seven pieces.

166. There are no Es in the passage. Nor are there any in the remaining 50,000 words of the book, which was published in 1939.

167. 250,500 cms, or 2505m, or 2.505km.
Basically, we want the answer to :

$$2 \times (1 + 2 + 3 + \ldots + 499 + 500)$$
$$= 2 \times (250 \times 501)$$

since the number in the bracket is just 250 pairs of 501 (pair together the numbers from either end).

168. Never, because the left pendulum is to the right of its swing at 6, 12, 18, 24, 30... seconds. The right pendulum is to the left of its swing at 5, 15, 25, 35, 45... seconds. Since the first series never ends in 5 but the second series always ends in 5 the pendulums won't touch.

169. Because every March 27th Uncle Brian forgets to put his clock forward an hour at 1am!

170. The answer is shown below :

171. The word MILL, to give Sugar mill, Flour mill, Wool mill, Pepper mill.

172. 5:19pm. From the two pieces of information we deduce that the fraction of the journey that took an hour is :

$$\frac{2}{3} - \frac{1}{4} = \frac{8}{12} - \frac{3}{12} = \frac{5}{12}$$

Therefore the whole journey took :

$$\frac{(12 \times 60)}{5} = 144 \text{ minutes}$$

Now, as a quarter of 144 is 36, he must have set off at 2:55, so he arrived 144 minutes later at 5:19.

173. Roll them – the faster one is solid.

174. These letters look similar whether in lower case or capitals, whereas other letters look different (A and a, for instance).

175. Two times. The outer ball rotates four times, the inner twice.

176. The valid words are : arm, ear, eye, gum, gut, hip, jaw, leg, lip, rib, toe.

177. 2.25.

178. Yes :

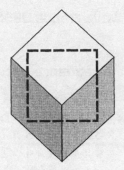

179. Deborah was born in Cambridge, Massachusetts, USA; Katherine was born in Cambridge, England.

180. 25%, or one-in-four. The colours were a clue. Since EACH board has 22 white, 21 grey and 21 black squares, and since each triple domino covers one white, one grey and one black square (no matter where it is) then the uncovered square must be white on BOTH boards. Thus the only ones this could be are the four marked below :

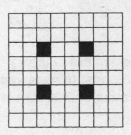

ANSWERS TO LAP 19

181. STRESSED, which reads DESSERTS backwards.

182. 7, because the sequence goes :

$$1 \times 1 \times 1 \times 1 \times 1 \times 1 \times 1 = 1$$
$$2 \times 2 \times 2 \times 2 \times 2 \times 2 = 64$$
$$3 \times 3 \times 3 \times 3 \times 3 = 243$$
$$4 \times 4 \times 4 \times 4 = 256$$
$$5 \times 5 \times 5 = 125$$
$$6 \times 6 = 36$$
$$7 = 7$$

183. (a). Since they are of equal mass they will rise at the same speed.

184. By lying along one corner of the square corridor. A 30 foot boulder leaves a 5 foot gap on each side which is comfortably wider than Illinois's shoulders.

185. The picture would be :

The pictures represent the planets of the solar system and their moons. (Notice that Neptune is number nine, because until 1999 it is farther out than Pluto.)

186. EIGHTH, which is an anagram of HEIGHT. All the words in the box have anagrams (eg. VETOED = DEVOTE, GRUDGE = RUGGED, etc.).

187. The result is nearly always 9. The "x18" ensures that the result is a multiple of nine, and therefore the digit sum will always be nine. The trick does not work in the rare instance that the result you get before the "x18" is zero.

188. 44, since it happens twice every hour (giving 48) but there are only three between 2 to 4, and 8 to 10, so 4 has to be subtracted.

189. 8; each number represents the number of letters in each word of the question.

190. Three of the shaded blocks move in the directions shown, so the fourth picture is :

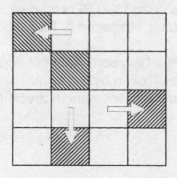

191. Anything that rhymes with NINE (such as a MINE, a PINE tree, a bottle of WINE etc.), since the other pictures rhyme with the numbers from one to eight (Gun, Shoe, Tree, etc.)

192. The three thousand, four hundred and seventieth, because :

$$(9^3 \times 4) + (9^2 \times 6) + (9 \times 7) + 5 = 3470$$

This is the standard method for working out a number using base 9.

193. (B). Using the formula for the area of a circle :

Total volume = no. of pipes $\times \pi \times$ radius^2

(A) $1 \times \pi 4^2 = 16\pi$
(B) $2 \times \pi 3^2 = 18\pi$
(C) $3 \times \pi 2^2 = 12\pi$

194. He was born in 1340 BC and died in 1322 BC, 18 years later. His name is Tut'ankhamun!

195. 18. The number represents the number of straight lines multiplied by the number of areas. The final figure has 6 lines and 3 areas, hence 6 x 3 = 18.

196. They are words that contain a Q that is NOT followed by U, namely Aqaba, Iraqi, Qadaffi, Qadi, Qantas, Qatar, Qintar, Qoph.

197. 0.8571429. They are the results shown on a calculator display for the following fractions :

$$\frac{1}{2}, \frac{2}{3}, \frac{3}{4}, \frac{4}{5}, \frac{5}{6}, \frac{6}{7}.$$

198. The cylinder – clearly the sphere or cone can fit into the cylinder so this must be largest.

199. It is an anagram of THE MAMMOTH BOOK OF BRAINSTORMING PUZZLES.

200. Four. The three dimensional solid that has vertices all equidistant from one another is the triangle-based pyramid. If you imagine this inscribed inside a ball, the four points touching the ball indicate the positions for the bases.

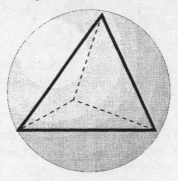

201. The longest I found were 5 letters long (including FLASK, FLASH, FLAGS) although there may be more obscure words depending on which dictionary you use.

202. Vicky does. In the second race, they meet at 10 metres from the finish line, so (as Vicky is the faster runner) she then gains a small lead before taking the tape.

203. It's an easy piece of geometry. The cards are slightly trapezium-shaped (see diagram). When the victim examines her card, Andrew turns the pack around. When Sylvia puts the card back in the pack, Andrew's fingers will automatically lift the card out of the pack.

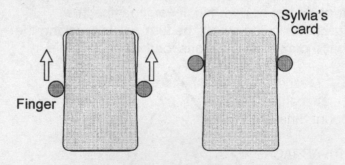

Sylvia's card

Finger

204. "BDC" is the odd one out – the other pieces pair up to form the words ABACUS, GERMAN and CANDLE when fitted together.

205. Here's how we did it, though there are other possible ways :

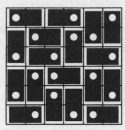

206. DODECAGON, a twelve-sided shape.

207. One way is : top number 7; second row 3, then 1, then 4; third row 5 then 8 then 6; bottom number 2.

208. When water boils, it stays exactly at boiling point forever until all the water has boiled away into steam. So, the Professor should make his coffee now while there still is water in the kettle.

209. Moses! (Geddit? – he took the two stone tablets containing the Ten Commandments from Mount Sinai.)

210. ABRACADABRA.

211. The unclued word is SOLVED. The answers are : Across – 2) Yes, 4) Nap, 6) Slur, 8) Umber, 12) Niece, 13) Cake, 14) Lop, 15) Nee; Down – 1) Census, 3) Salmon, 5) Public, 7) Reveal, 9) Reckon, 11) Deepen.

212. Top row : 1 + 7 / 2; middle row : 6 x 5 – 8; bottom row 4 x 9 – 3.

213. 5 scratches in total, since diamond scratches all three tiles, quartz scratches copper and gypsum, and talc is the softest so doesn't scratch anything.

214. Italy drives on the right-hand side of the road, so should be placed on the right of the line.

215. Since the total of the numbers is 32, and two lines crossing makes four sections, then each partition contains a total of 8.

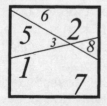

216. The final answer is GERMAN MANGER. The answers to the individual clues are :
1) EMIT time, 2) SNUG gnus, 3) LEMON melon, 4) Norse SENOR, 5) SWORE worse, 6) SPORADIC Picadors. The words in capitals are the ones you should have put into the grid.

217. A, because this makes all the rows and columns add up to 20.

218. Birds can't swallow food or water without gravity. Humans can swallow when doing handstands since we have muscles that contract to force things down, but birds don't have this ability.

219. A native French speaker who can touch-type. The culprit killed Jack in the dark, then touch-typed a message onto the screen. However, the French use a keyboard whose top line begins AZERTY whereas Jack was using the standard QWERTY keyboard.

220. The riddle reads "What has no wings, no rotors and yet can fly?" Turn the book 90 degrees, look at what you have traced and the answer becomes obvious!

221. The words are WATT, ZONED, TUNNEL, ZEPHYR and WOUNDED.

222. Square the number then take away twice the original number. In equation form :

$$Output = Input^2 - (2 \times Input)$$

223. B – it's not as hard as it looks. Move the black dot through the maze-like structure until it's outside. Only in B does the dot come out between the arrows.

224. Canada is 4, since there are four geometric shapes on its national flag, two red rectangles, a white rectangle and the maple leaf. So, for example, this explains why the USA is 64 (50 stars, the blue rectangle which contains the stars, and 13 stripes).

225. Across – ITS, CADET, ARENA, READY, AS; Down – CAR, AREA, IDEAS, TEND, STAY.

226. I boasted that I could form the word BIGHEAD.

227. 10 (representing X). The common Roman numerals have been put into alphabetical order – C, D, I, L, M, V, X.

228. The words SQUARE NUMBER can be read after just two twists of the cube :

Read here

229. The man had been doing nothing wrong by burning pieces of meaningless cloth. However, he happened to be in Libya, where the national flag is a plain green rectangle. By burning it he had offended the crowd and broken the law.

230. A picture of an angel.

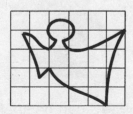

231. The anagram is DIAGRAM.
Across – 1) Stem, 5) Tide, 6) Alga, 7) Reed; Down
– 1) Star, 2) Tile, 3) Edge, 4) Mead.

232. Place "b" down first, then put "a" on top, then
"c" on top of that. This will make the sum read : 33
x 29 = 297 + 660 = 957.

233. The reason is due to the peculiarities of the
hour hand. You can always tell where 12 o'clock is
by noting the only place where both the hour and
minute hand point to the same hour marking. If
you accidentally mistake 3 o'clock for 12 o'clock,
the hands would not align properly.

234. This is a lateral thinking question for a good
reason. If you use Roman numerals (with C in the
circles, X in the diamonds, and I in the triangles)
everything becomes clear...

235. The answer relies on counting the black (as
well as white) sections.

236. ATMOSPHERIC can be spelt out.

237. The record has several interleaved grooves. The diagram shows one track, the others are similar spirals using the gaps.

238. A and B fit together if one of them is turned upside-down. If you thought A and C fit together, the block marked here prevents this.

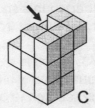

239. It reads "Congratulations, you have solved it". You probably got the answer by looking at alternate letters, but this code was traditionally read by winding the paper strip around a pole. Try it for yourself!

240. I reckon you need to move 8 mirrors (in black). Notice the use of both sides of one mirror near the bottom of the course. The fact that the path crosses doesn't matter either, since laser light does not interfere with itself when crossing.

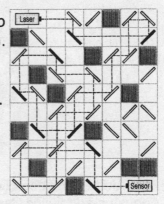

241. Across – 4) Bauxite, 6) Ace, 7) Oatmeal, 9) Lei, 10) Granite; Down – 1) Cavalry, 2) Examine, 3) Stealth, 5) Ice, 8) Tea.

242. The fence posts will have to be next to each other! In this situation the six-foot long chain is only one foot from the ground.

243. There is a circle, radius $10 + \frac{5}{\pi}$ miles from the South Pole, which satisfies the condition, as you will see from the diagram. (In fact, depending on how many times you circle the pole, there are other answers.)

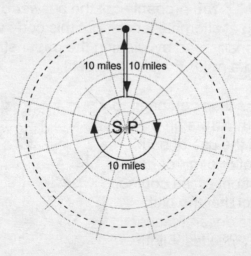

244. Ten months became twelve in honour of Augustus and Julius Caesar in 44 BC.

245. The answer is 42. Hands up all those who thought the answer was 44 (=396 / 9). If so, you overlooked the fact that after the 42nd square you are left with a useless 1 x 18 inch strip.

246. The newspaper headline is a palindrome (that is, it can be read backwards and forwards as the same thing).

247. The full list is infinitely long, but the pattern starts 1 and 0, 2 and –1, 3 and –2, 4 and –3, 5 and –4, 6 and –5, and so on. The mathematical way to solve the problem is :

$$x^2 - x = y^2 - y$$
$$x(x-1) = y(y-1)$$

Therefore $x = 1 - y$

or $x = 0$, $y = 0$ (not allowed)

so $x = 1 - y$ is the formula to use.

248. It will be 4.5 units long. This is because the springs are normally 1.5 units long, and the weight stretches them by one unit. However, the combination of springs in the diagram makes the extension 1.5 times longer. Hence the answer is 3 + (1.5 x 1) = 4.5 units.

249. A ghost train or other theme-park ride.

250. 46 (28 edges plus 18 faces.)

ROUND 1 PROGRESS CHART

Plot your scores on the chart and see if you are keeping up with the target to beat.

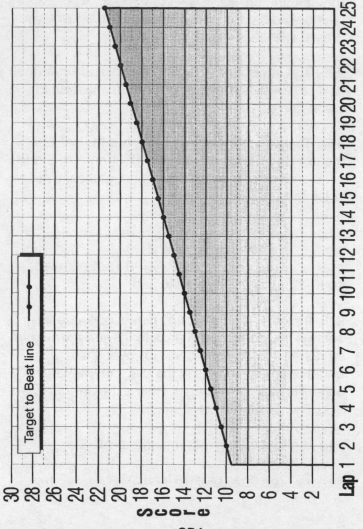

254

ROUND 2

Having tested you thoroughly in all aspects logical, visual, numerical, technological and verbal, we now go further. If you have worked through Round 1 before reaching this point you probably found the puzzles there quite abstract in that they rarely required any previous general knowledge – I now allow myself this extra luxury.

However to compensate for this extra requirement you will find that Round 2 is far less sneaky – no nasty tricks, no hidden clues, just a set of interesting puzzles for you to play with.

Another concession this time is that there are no time limits. This is because there is more of an element of "you know it or you don't" so there seems little point in applying time pressure, especially as these puzzles will take you longer to complete.

The format is different too. There are ten kinds of puzzles, one of each kind appearing in every Lap. You will find that as you get used to the games there will be a number of tactical observations you can make to help you solve each puzzle. For example, with the In the Pipeline puzzles you can answer the questions to fill the grid, yet you can also deduce things from the grid to help you answer the questions. This interesting two-way process is a feature of many of the puzzles that follow.

There are no stars in this Round. Instead, each
game has a different scoring system, and these
are described in the following pages. Again, no
points are lost for incorrect answers and you can
use the first page of each Lap to record your
scores.

I have been careful in my selection of material for
puzzles using general knowledge questions. I trust
that all readers, no matter where they live, will be
fairly familiar with the scope of knowledge used.
This balancing act means that you might find
some "easy" questions – ones which other readers
might not find so straightforward. Of course, the
converse is bound to happen and I hope I have
crafted the book such that it happens equally as
often. Enough said.

There are still the "Target To Beat" targets set at
the start of each lap, so bear these in mind. There
is another progress chart at the end of the round,
together with the "Final Reckoning" page where
you can finally evaluate your performance.

So, before commencing battle with the puzzles
themselves, it would be worth your while spending
a few minutes familiarising yourself with the
instructions that follow.

INSTRUCTIONS FOR ROUND 2

1   QUIZWORD

The first type of game in each lap is a crossword with a difference. Each clue is a trivia question, the answer to which should be entered into the grid in the usual fashion. Interlocking letters should provide you with extra clues for those questions that you cannot answer straight away.

You score 1 point for every clue you manage to complete correctly, up to a maximum of 25 points. You may NOT score more even if you have achieved higher than this. There are around 30 clues in each Quizword.

2   REBUS CHALLENGE

You will notice that the icon for this game is a bus with "RE" on it. In other words, it's a RE-bus. Rebus – get it? This is typical of the type of puzzle you'll be dealing with here. A rebus is a pictorial representation of a popular phrase or saying which you have to find. It won't be straightforward – the colour, positioning, shape or style of the lettering or pictures are used in clever ways to provide extra "cryptic-ness".

So, for example, suppose you were given the following rebus to solve :

BEELZEBUB C VIOLET

– – – – – – –   – – –   – – – – –   – – –

– – –   – – – –   – – – –   – – –

Well, Beelzebub is another name for the Devil, and violet is a shade of blue, and there is the letter C between them. Perhaps the answer is "Between the devil and the deep blue sea" (since between the devil and the deep blue there is "C"). Notice that homophones (words that sound the same although spelled differently) are often used, so watch out for them. Also watch out for arrows – they usually point out something very important in the puzzle.

You get five points for every correctly identified rebus, there being six in each Lap, so the top score on this game is 30 points. The dashes can be used to check your answer.

3   SAFE CRACKER

The third game is Safe Cracker. You are presented with ten statements, a number of which are falsehoods. For each statement decide whether it is true or false. Then, for all the FALSE statements, shade in those segments in the digital display that are coded with this letter. For example, if you decide that statements A, G, H and K are all false, then shade in all segments bearing the letter A, G, H or K.

If you have done the puzzle correctly, the segments that you have shaded in will form a correct sum (as shown) and you've cracked the combination to the safe.

There are no points for doing this as such, but you are awarded two points for every statement whose truth (or otherwise) you establish correctly.

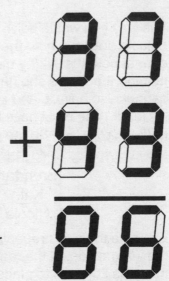

259

LOGIC PROBLEM

A Logic Problem is a puzzle asking you to deduce a situation from a number of given clues. As an example, suppose we have three children called Kath, Nicola and Brendan. They each hold a different letter on a piece of card, either N, B or K. Now suppose we are given the following :

(1) No child holds a card bearing the same letter as the first letter of their name.
(2) Nicola does not hold a card with 'B' on it.

The way you would solve this is as follows :
"Nicola does not hold the 'B' (by clue 2) and she cannot hold the 'N' (by clue 1) so she must be holding the 'K'. As she has the 'K' then Brendan cannot also have it, and since he cannot have the 'B' (clue 1) he must have the 'N', hence leaving Kath with the 'B'." So the solution is :

Child	Letter
Brendan	N
Kath	B
Nicola	K

Examine the clues repeatedly until you deduce all the information. In the real puzzles you will have as many as 20 items to place, and you get 1 point for every piece of information you put into the correct place in the answer grid.

IN THE PIPELINE

The best way to demonstrate the In the Pipeline puzzles is to do an example. The rectangular grid shows both ends of three pipes.

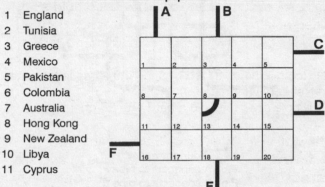

1 England
2 Tunisia
3 Greece
4 Mexico
5 Pakistan
6 Colombia
7 Australia
8 Hong Kong
9 New Zealand
10 Libya
11 Cyprus

In the full puzzle there would be a list of twenty items on the left (in this case, countries) each of which uses one of the terms below to describe their unit of currency.

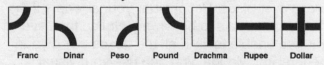

Franc   Dinar   Peso   Pound   Drachma   Rupee   Dollar

For each item in the list, draw the appropriate diagram in the numbered square. For example, if question 13 is FRANCE which has the Franc as its currency, draw the symbol corresponding to Franc in box number 13 (as shown above).

261

If you correctly repeat this for the other 19 squares, the diagram will show you how the pipe ends connect together.

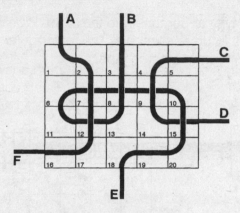

Your answer :
Pipe A connects to pipe F
Pipe B connects to pipe E
Pipe C connects to pipe D

The aim of the game is to deduce how the pipes connect up (as shown above). The three pipes never join, but may pass over other pipes via the cross-over piece. Reconsider your answers if the diagram appears to be wrong. Notice that, even if you are unable to fill in all the boxes using your general knowledge, you can use your visual intuition of the diagram to help you. I'll leave you to discover these tricks for yourself.

You get one point for every square correctly drawn into the diagram.

6   MYSTERY STORY

Here you are given a mystery story which has a question at the end. Using your powers of detection, and perhaps some logical and lateral thought in the process, it is up to you to answer the question with the right reason behind your answer. 25 points are yours if you can do this.

7   WORD ISLAND

In Word Island, you have to form words of five letters or more by travelling from state to state around our island. For each word you may start anywhere you like, passing through touching borders to pick up the next letter (which you MUST do – skipping states isn't allowed). For example, if we were travelling around the island of Verbia

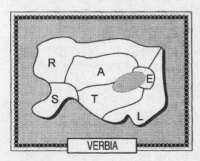

VERBIA

shown here, then the words LETTER, TASTERS, STARE and RATTLE are fine, but LASTS is not. Note that double letters (picking up a letter twice when in a state) are OK, as are plurals.

To help you with ten of the longest words we've provided clues, so for our example you might be given :

 Do they test tea?

 Percussion for a snake

After that you are on your own to find up to another 20 five letter words in a similar fashion. You score 1 point for every word you find, up to the maximum of 30, no matter whether it's one of the clued words or one you've found yourself.

8   MISSING LINKS

Game 8, Missing Links, is a lateral thinking puzzle. We provide you with six clues each pointing towards a person, object, place or event. However, the clues are coded using a simple cipher. To decode, simply write down the letters next in alphabetical order to those printed. So, for example, if the clue says "CZUHC I. ANCXBNLAD" then decoded it reads "DAVID J. BODYCOMBE". Notice that Z is used to represent the letter A.

Begin by decoding the top clue. Think about what it could point towards, and if anything comes to mind write it in the right-hand box beside it, under "Guesses".

Now decode the second clue, and make another guess if anything different comes to mind. Continue by decoding every clue and making one guess after each clue. The following shows a game in progress, in this case to identify a famous person (shown by the WHO? banner at the top).

WHO?	GUESSES
EHUD FIVE	ENID BLYTON 12
AZC = FNNC BAD = GOOD	10
BZLDQZ RGX? CAMERA SHY?	MICHAEL JACKSON 8
LNNMVZKJ MOONWALK	6
ATAAKDR	4
SGQHKKDQ	2

When this player checks his answers he will find that he guessed the correct answer after three clues and thus scores 8 points (shown by the number in that box). There are four of these games in each Lap and you should add up the four scores you get, up to a maximum of 30 points. On average, you'll probably get the right answer after the fourth clue – guessing it before then is good going. (You might like to decode the last two clues in the above grid for practice.)

265

9   NUMEROLOGY

This is a quiz about numbers. The catch is... you won't know half of the answers! You are given ten questions, labelled A to K, the answer to each being a number between 1 and 500. Half of them are fairly typical general knowledge or trivia questions. However, the other half ask you to estimate the number. The challenge is to use your knowledge to make a reasonable guess at the answer. For example, if the question was :

"How many tonnes did the largest ever bell, the Tsar Kolokol, weigh?"

at this point you might well think 'How on earth am I supposed to know that?' The idea is – you're not. However, you might know that a family car weighs around 1000kg (a tonne) and since bells are pretty big things perhaps the answer is around 120? Actually, the answer is 202 but at least we got fairly close. Some answers are easier to ascertain than others.

Once you've got your answers, put your answer for A in the box with A in it on the right-hand page, and likewise for the other letters. Then calculate the sums in the manner demonstrated on the next page.

RUNNING
TOTALS

| A 120 | × | B 3 | = | 360 |

TOTAL SO FAR + C 45 = 405

TOTAL SO FAR − D 95 = 310

Then follow the instructions given in the puzzle to work out how far away your final answer is from the correct answer. Award yourself the number of points according to the following scheme :

Difference between 0 and 250 = score 25 pts
Difference between 251 and 1000 = score 20 pts
Difference between 1001 and 2500 = score 15 pts
Difference between 2501 and 5000 = score 10 pts
Difference between 5001 and 7500 = score 5 pts

NOTES

(a) Your running total should always lie between 1 and 10,000 so if you go outside this region in your calculations you might like to reconsider your answers.

(b) Figures used in this quiz come from various sources, but in all cases the latest available information has been used.

(c) Sometimes figures have been rounded to the nearest whole number.

#10 MAGNIFICENT MAZE

In this maze you have to earn the moves you make. You do this by answering the twelve general knowledge questions provided. Check with the back of the book to see how many answers you got right. This is the number of moves you are allowed.

Starting at either S square, use your moves to trace the path through the maze, following the arrows at all times. If you come to a dead end, that's the end of your scoring. You score the number of points that you have managed to collect using your moves (see example). Once you have visited a circle, it counts as zero on subsequent visits, as in this example :

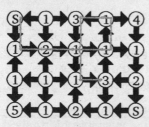

Suppose I got nine questions right. Using my nine moves as shown, I would have scored :
1+2+1+1+1+3+0+1+3
= 13 points

The following couple of pages give a summary of how to score your performance for the games in each Lap.

QUIZWORD
1 point for each clue correctly entered into the crossword.
Maximum score – 25 points

REBUS CHALLENGE
5 points for each rebus correctly identified.
Maximum score – 30 points

SAFE CRACKER
2 points for correctly identifying whether each statement is true or false.
Maximum score – 20 points

LOGIC PROBLEM
1 point for each correct piece of information entered into the answer grid.
Maximum score – 20 points

IN THE PIPELINE
1 point for each correct square of the pipeline entered into the grid.
Maximum score – 20 points

CRIME STORY

Solve the mystery with the correct reason to get the points, otherwise score zero.
Maximum score – 25 points

WORD ISLAND

1 point each for words with clues;
1 point each for up to 20 more valid words found.
Maximum score – 30 points

MISSING LINKS

Score the number of points shown in the box where you first wrote the correct answer (e.g. 8 points if you guessed the answer after clue 3).
Maximum score – 30 points

NUMEROLOGY

Score the number of points shown in the table, depending on how close you were to the answer.
Maximum score – 25 points

MAGNIFICENT MAZE

Score the points you collect using the moves you have earned.
Maximum score – 25 points

LAP 26

There are no time limits on this lap.

To score each puzzle, refer to the summary on pages 269–270. The maximum scores available are shown below.

	MAX.	SCORE
QUIZWORD	25	
REBUS CHALLENGE	30	
SAFE CRACKER	20	
LOGIC PROBLEM	20	
IN THE PIPELINE	20	
CRIME STORY	25	
WORD ISLAND	30	
MISSING LINKS	30	
NUMEROLOGY	25	
MAGNIFICENT MAZE	25	
TOTAL (max. 250)		

TARGET TO BEAT – 80 points

ACROSS

1 For which 1979 Vietnam War epic did Francis Ford Coppola win an Academy award? (10,3)

8 Which ancient city of Crete was home to the Minotaur's labyrinth in Greek mythology? (7)

9 What term describes a test screening of a film designed to gauge audience reaction? (7)

11 Which tropical member of the gourd family is often used for cleaning the skin? (6)

13 Lasting a period of 365 days? (8)

15 What word describes long regions of hair found on the necks of many animals, especially horses, lions and wolves? (5)

16 Offenbach composed the operetta _____ *in the Underworld* in 1858 (7)

18 What type of church was first founded by the Englishmen Smyth and Helwys in Amsterdam in 1609? (7)

19 Which type of flesh-eating demon takes on the form of a beautiful woman? (5)

21 In psychology, this type of therapy uses a stimulus (such as electric shocks) to dissuade someone from a bad habit? (8)

23 In printing, this describes a slanted form of lettering (6)

25 What type of military settlement is stationed far from the main camp? (7)

26 What form of gliding dance, a fore-runner of the fox-trot, is set to music with two beats in the bar? (3-4)

28 Which famous Belgian detective dies in the 1975 murder mystery novel *Curtain*? (7,6)

DOWN

2 In English, which part of speech can be either personal, demonstrative, interrogative or indefinite? (7)

3 What mathematical function is the ratio of the adjacent side to the hypotenuse in a right-angled triangle? (abbrev.) (3)

4 Which computer language derives its name from the abbreviation for List Processing? (4)

5 In *Monty Python's Flying Circus* what was the collective name for the strange-talking women portrayed by the cast? (10)

6 What title is given to certain chiefs in North Africa and also all those descending from Mohammed? (5)

7 Anything portending evil is said to be this (7)

8 Which mountain, situated in Tanzania, is the highest in Africa? (11)

10 What trophy is competed for in the annual matches between women tennis players of the USA and Britain? (8,3)

12 Which Greek slave from Phrygia wrote fables in the 6th Century BC? (5)

14 In economics, what type of merger brings together firms from the same level in the production chain? (10)

17 What word for "a striking effect" derives from the French word *éclater*, meaning "to shine"? (5)

18 Which word is more commonly used to mean "respire" when pertaining to humans? (7)

20 What is the name given to someone who has a Negro parent and a Caucasian parent? (7)

22 What school of philosophy was founded in Athens by Zeno in 300 BC? (5)

24 In organ music, what mechanism is used to prevent a given row of pipes from sounding? (4)

27 What is the French word for "yes"? (3)

1

BLOOD
H_2O

_ _ _ _ _ _ _ _ _ _ _ _ _ _
_ _ _ _ _ _ _ _ _

   2

_ _ _ _ _ _ _ _ _ _

   3

_ _ _ _ _ _ _ _ _ _ _ _ _ _ _

274

4

--- ----------

5

--- ---- ----

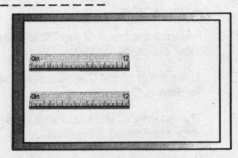

6

BSc MA PhD

----- ------ ----

Blacken out those segments on the right-hand page that are letter coded to the FALSE statements. This will form a correct mathematical sum.

		True	False
A	e.g. stands for exempli gratia	☐	☐
B	Matthias is the Apostle who replaced Judas Iscariot	☐	☐
C	Isaiah is the book of the Bible with the most chapters, at 150	☐	☐
D	The capital of the Canadian province Toronto is Ontario	☐	☐
E	The country of Burkino Faso was once also called Abyssinia	☐	☐
F	Polyhymnia was the Greek Muse of song and dance	☐	☐
G	Mount Logan is the highest mountain in Canada	☐	☐
H	St Joseph is the patron saint of travellers	☐	☐
J	The Statue of Zeus, a Wonder of the World, was situated in Athens	☐	☐
K	The first underground railway system was built in London	☐	☐

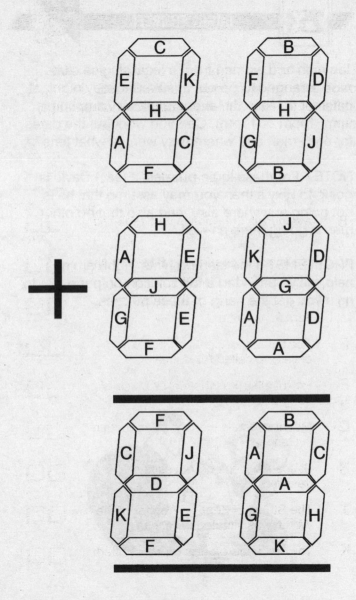

277

LOGIC PROBLEM

Ten men and women from a local singles club have arranged to go out this Wednesday night, at different times in the evening (either 7pm, 8pm, 9pm, 10pm or 11pm). Can you work out the dates for each man and where they went at what time?

NOTE – For these logic puzzles, if (say) David is going to Rixy's then you may assume that he is not going anywhere else, and also that no other man is going there as well.

PROBLEMS? If the starting hints (right) are no help, we've provided a full solution on page 474 to help you get the hang of these puzzles.

CLUES

1. Katherine's date will be the latest, at 11pm. It won't be with Dan, nor will it be to the cinema.

2. Mary wants to go ice skating before 8:30pm.

3. The couple who plan to go out drinking at the New Inn will do so at 7pm.

4. Patrick and Victoria will make a lovely couple on Wednesday.

5. David is off to Rixy's for a spot of clubbing.

6. Simon is going out with his date at 8pm.

7. Jane will be going out an hour before Patrick. She doesn't like videos.

8. The 11pm daters won't be watching a video either.

9. Dan and Jane are not going out together.

STARTING HINTS

a. Use clues 2, 3 and 6 to deduce when Mary went skating and with whom. Use this information together with clues 4 and 7 to see why Jane could not have gone to the New Inn at 7pm. Deduce which woman did go there. Now...

b. Use clue 2 to see when Patrick and Jane will go out.

c. Who is going out with Jill (the fifth woman)? Who is watching the video?

Man	Woman	Venue	Time
Dan			
Dave			
David			
Patrick			
Simon			

Your task is to associate each of the following scientific words with the subject with which they are most readily associated.

1. Protractor
2. Filter funnel
3. Dolomite
4. Icosahedron
5. Culture
6. Red dwarf
7. Streptococcus
8. Compiler
9. Flowchart
10. Anemometer
11. Isotherm
12. Quadratic
13. Litmus paper
14. Substratum
15. Moraine
16. Galaxy
17. ROM
18. Gamete
19. Liebig condenser
20. Feldspar

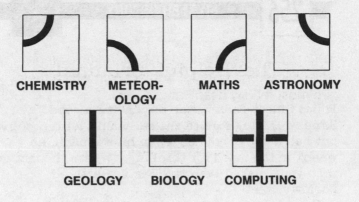

CHEMISTRY **METEOR-OLOGY** **MATHS** **ASTRONOMY**

GEOLOGY **BIOLOGY** **COMPUTING**

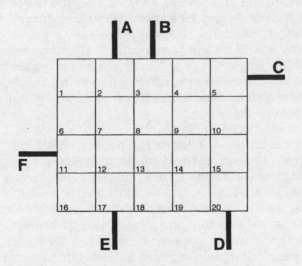

Your answer :

Pipe __ connects to pipe __

Pipe __ connects to pipe __

Pipe __ connects to pipe __

The 'Helpful' Criminal

Police Officer Barlow was not having a good Sunday. Having started the early shift with nothing but half a cup of cold coffee in his stomach, he wasn't in the mood for thinking. "What's the matter with you?" asked Detective Frank Hartland, Barlow's chief.

"One of the juniors has given me details of some tip-offs that Smiley Pete wants us to look into," explained Barlow.

"Why would he want to do that?" Hartland asked.

"He has his court case tomorrow so I suppose he wants to put word around that he's being helpful." Barlow walked over to the filing cabinet and pulled out Smiley Pete's file.

"Try me," offered Hartland.

Barlow shuffled through the papers. "Well, he claims he knows of three pieces of stolen property that the world hasn't found out about yet. Firstly he claims that the actual musical scores on which Irving Berlin composed 'Annie Get Your Gun' are missing. He said that some criminals he knows stole them from a museum of music in New York last year, but since there are so many documents there the theft hasn't been discovered yet."

"Hmm. OK, what else did he say?" The Detective began to think as Barlow read out the second claim.

"He then went on to say that a criminal gang had, just yesterday, stolen the Codex of Leonardo da

Vinci's inventions. He said that he's seen it personally and that the descriptions of things such as the helicopter are in clear Italian and are unmistakable. And wait for it..."

"Well, you might as well cap this lie." Hartland allowed himself a wide smile.

"He claims that his partner-in-crime sneaked into the Louvre yesterday morning before the galleries opened posing as a postman. This man is supposed to have smuggled out the 'Mona Lisa' in a rolled up postal tube! The thing is, I don't want to be the one who's ridiculed if any of these stories turn out to be true."

"I'd consider charging him for wasting police time if all those stories weren't so hopelessly funny!" chuckled Hartland.

Can you point out to Barlow the exact reason why at least two of the above stories are wrong?

Clues to ten of the longest words that we managed to find :

1	*Expected next*
2	*Hated*
3	*Bonhomie, ____ cordiale?*
4	*Hat made from felt, for men*
5	*Relaxed French attitude*
6	*Singularity*
7	*Indicates, stands for*
8	*Shakespeare's poems*
9	*Sofas, easy chairs*
10	*Captured at the rodeo?*

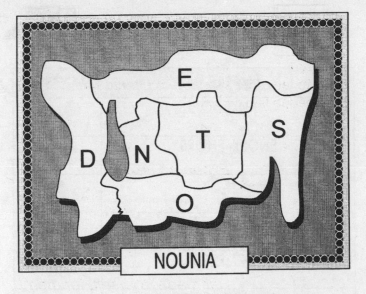

NOUNIA

Other words of five letters or more (find up to another 20) :

WHO?	GUESSES
FNKEDQ	12
ENQSX–EHQRS	10
B.H.Z.	8
QDOTAKHBZM	6
HQZMFZSD	4
MN LNQD SZWDR	2

WHAT?	GUESSES
MDV HM DHFGSX-SVN	12
KDZCHMF ENQLZS	10
SVDKUD BL CHZLDSDQ	8
CHFHSZK	6
KZRDQ KHFGS	4
RSNQDR LTRHB	2

WHERE?	GUESSES
EKZSSDRS	12
BNLOTKRNQX RTEEQZFD	10
DHFGS RSZSDR	8
MNSZAKD NODQZ UDMTD	6
RNZO NODQZ BNTMSQX	4
FQDZS AZQQHDQ QDDE	2

WHEN?	GUESSES
KDC AX QNADQS BZSDRAX	12
BNMROHQZBX AX BZSGNKHBR	10
ZSSDLOS NM IZLDR H	8
EHQDVNQJR	6
EHESG NE MNUDLADQ	4
FTX EZVJDR ZQQDRSDC	2

For each of the statements below, put your guesstimated answer in the appropriate box on the opposite page.

A How old was Tutankhamun when he died?

B How many permanent members are there in the UN Security Council?

C How many kilometres long is the longest road tunnel in the world?

D How many pieces are on a chessboard at the start of a game?

E How many inches high is a men's 100m hurdle?

F How many standard ballet positions are there?

G The summer solstice takes place on June _?_ in the Northern Hemisphere.

H How many minutes did the first ever spacewalk last?

J What was the % turnout at the 1984 US Presidential election?

K What percentage of the Earth's surface is covered by water?

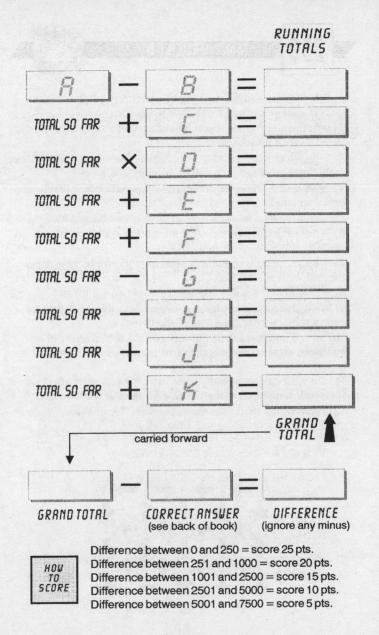

RUNNING TOTALS

A	−	B	=	
TOTAL SO FAR	+	C	=	
TOTAL SO FAR	×	D	=	
TOTAL SO FAR	+	E	=	
TOTAL SO FAR	+	F	=	
TOTAL SO FAR	−	G	=	
TOTAL SO FAR	−	H	=	
TOTAL SO FAR	+	J	=	
TOTAL SO FAR	+	K	=	

GRAND TOTAL

carried forward

| | − | | = | |
| GRAND TOTAL | | CORRECT ANSWER (see back of book) | | DIFFERENCE (ignore any minus) |

HOW TO SCORE

Difference between 0 and 250 = score 25 pts.
Difference between 251 and 1000 = score 20 pts.
Difference between 1001 and 2500 = score 15 pts.
Difference between 2501 and 5000 = score 10 pts.
Difference between 5001 and 7500 = score 5 pts.

1) Which film, with the working title of *A Boy's Life*, had three midget stars whose real faces were never seen?

2) What would you see if you looked up close at a picture painted in the style of pointillism?

3) With which other country does Jordan share a sea that contains eight times more salt than that of ordinary sea water?

4) What was the name of the original super-continent that later broke up into Laurasia and Gondwanaland?

5) Which weapon would a Roman have called his *gladius*?

6) What can basenjis not do that most other breeds of this animal can?

7) A fax machine is commonly used in modern everyday office life but what is "fax" short for?

8) Which organ contains two auricles and two ventricles?

9) What is the name of the twin sons of Zeus and Leda that are depicted in star charts as Gemini, the twins?

10) Which unit, used in metallurgy and the manufacture of jewellery, signifies the proportion of precious metal to base metal?

11) On what subject would you be expert if you most often ask for a yellow question in the Genus edition of *Trivial Pursuit*?

12) From which sport does the expression "Go for Gold" come, the aim of the sport being to hit the yellow?

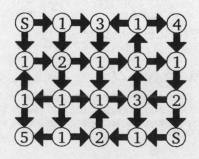

LAP 27

There are no time limits on this lap.

To score each puzzle, refer to the summary on pages 269–270. The maximum scores available are shown below.

	MAX.	SCORE
QUIZWORD	25	
REBUS CHALLENGE	30	
SAFE CRACKER	20	
LOGIC PROBLEM	20	
IN THE PIPELINE	20	
CRIME STORY	25	
WORD ISLAND	30	
MISSING LINKS	30	
NUMEROLOGY	25	
MAGNIFICENT MAZE	25	
TOTAL (max. 250)		

TARGET TO BEAT – 95 points

(crossword grid with numbered squares: 1, 2, 3, 4, 5, 6, 7, 8, 9, 10, 11, 12, 13, 14, 15, 16, 17, 18, 19, 20, 21, 22, 23, 24, 25, 26, 27, 28)

ACROSS

1 Which type of Chinese-style plate design was popularized in England by Mintons Ltd. in 1783? (6,7)

8 This word means "to reduce one's reserves" (7)

9 What, in the English language, is a statement used to express a generally accepted observation about everyday life? (7)

11 These are a type of knitted pullover, so-called due to their distinctive collar (1-5)

13 Which American missile contains a television camera which it uses to follow its target? (8)

15 A physicist might call it light amplification by stimulated emission of radiation. How is it more commonly known? (5)

16 In the field of insurance, what name is given to a regular amount of money paid to insure against possible larger losses? (7)

292

18 What Italian dish is made from envelopes of pasta stuffed with meat or cheese, usually served in a sauce? (7)

19 The best possible (5)

21 What geometric term is defined as "to draw a figure as large as possible inside another figure"? (8)

23 This architectural term means "to decorate with raised stone or wood work" (6)

25 What type of gas, commonly found near oil deposits, consists of a mixture of gases such as butane and propane? (7)

26 What title was given to an empress of Russia? (7)

28 What medical condition, formerly called mongolism, occurs due to the presence of three copies of chromosome 21? (5,8)

DOWN

2 Which word means "to print" and "to influence the mind"? (7)

3 The general who commanded the Confederacy during the American Civil War was Robert E. _____ (3)

4 Which small bird has the scientific name *Troglodytes troglodytes*? (4)

5 In what order is a lexicon usually arranged? (10)

6 Which demonstrative pronoun is the plural of "that"?

7 Which radioactive metallic element has the chemical symbol Re? (7)

8 In economics, what term describes the reduction of the home currency's exchange rate in the international money markets? (11)

10 What dessert is made from hot meringue filled with cold ice cream? (5,6)

12 To which Leningrad ballet company did Rudolf Nureyev belong? (5)

14 Which birds, similar to ibises, are distinguished by their flat beaks? (10)

17 What term describes a phrase particular to a given language that is a grammatical exception to normal reasoning – e.g. "a flight of stairs" doesn't fly? (5)

18 Which Italian dish is made from rice cooked with saffron, stock, meat, vegetables and/or cheese? (7)

20 What psychological condition is identified by an overuse of the word "I"? (7)

22 What word means "to repeat a radio or television broadcast" and "to repeat a race"? (5)

24 In computing, what word describes a small picture intended to represent a particular action, such as saving a file? (4)

27 What acronym is used to indicate the true interest rate, taking into account compound interest? (3)

1

___ _____ ___ _____

DIMENSION
DIMENSION
DIMENSION
DIMENSION

2

___ _____ _____

 3

_____ _____

294

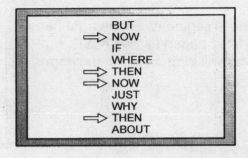

BUT
⇒ NOW
IF
WHERE
⇒ THEN
⇒ NOW
JUST
WHY
⇒ THEN
ABOUT

4

_____ ___ ___ ____

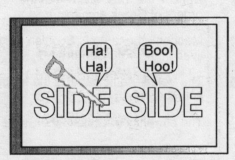

Ha!
Ha!

Boo!
Hoo!

SIDE   SIDE

5

___ ___ _____ ____

TERM

6

_ _ _ _ _ _ _ _ _ _ _ _ _ _ _

295

Blacken out those segments on the right-hand page that are letter coded to the FALSE statements. This will form a correct mathematical sum.

		True	False
A	Kochel numbers are assigned to classify the works of Beethoven	☐	☐
B	Doric is the most stylized of the three orders of Greek architecture	☐	☐
C	Macbeth, the famous Scottish king, lived in the 15th Century AD	☐	☐
D	The Volga–Baltic canal is the longest in the world	☐	☐
E	The currency of Chile is the Sucre	☐	☐
F	The Roman ruler Caligula made his horse, Incitatus, a Consul	☐	☐
G	*Sit Down You're Rocking the Boat* comes from the musical *Guys & Dolls*	☐	☐
H	St Michael is the patron saint of tax collectors	☐	☐
J	Shakespeare's *A Midsummer Night's Dream* is set in Rome	☐	☐
K	Princeton is the United States' oldest university	☐	☐

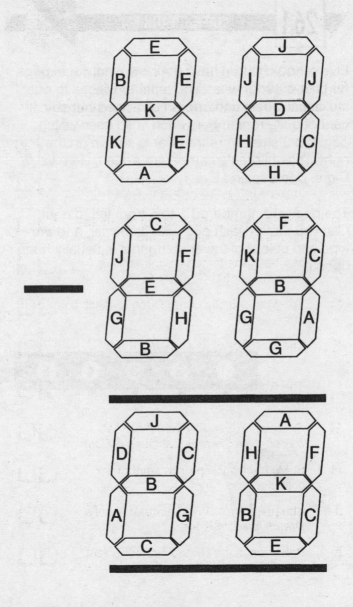

Five schoolchildren have their own individual pegs for their outdoor wear. The teacher wishes to put individual labels underneath each peg but she cannot quite remember which child uses which peg. What she can remember is shown on the right. The children's names are Adrian, Bernard, Clare, Dominic and Eve.

The pegs are numbered 1 to 5 from left to right. Can you match each peg with its owner, and the type and colour of the clothing that is usually hung upon it?

CLUES

1. Clare's anorak is somewhere to the left of the green duffel coat. However, these two garments are not directly side-by-side.

2. The clothing on peg 4 is blue, but it isn't a polo neck.

3. Eve's article of clothing is on peg 1. She does not wear the brown garment.

4. Bernard's clothing is black.

5. There is a raincoat on peg 3.

6. Adrian doesn't wear cardigans.

STARTING HINTS

a. Work out on which pegs Clare's anorak and the green duffel coat are.

b. Use the first four clues to find the colour of Eve's clothing.

c. On which peg is Bernard's black coat?

NOTES

The five articles are : an anorak, a cardigan, a duffel coat, a polo neck sweater, and a raincoat.

The five colours are : black, blue, brown, green and tan.

Peg	Child	Article	Colour
Number 1			
Number 2			
Number 3			
Number 4			
Number 5			

Your task is to put the breeds of animal below into the seven categories provided.

1 Anaconda

2 Marmoset

3 Gecko

4 Mandrill

5 Chihuahua

6 Schnauzer

7 Cariacou

8 Buzzard

9 Petrel

10 Whimbrel

11 Abyssinian

12 Iguana

13 Shrike

14 Chinchilla

15 Pomeranian

16 Palomino

17 Osprey

18 Corncrake

19 Clydesdale

20 Burmese

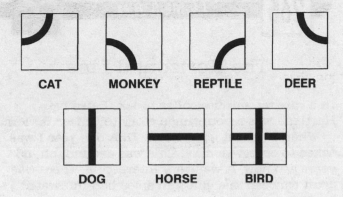

CAT **MONKEY** **REPTILE** **DEER**

DOG **HORSE** **BIRD**

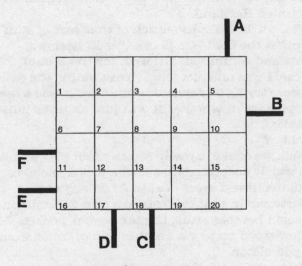

Your answer :
Pipe __ connects to pipe __
Pipe __ connects to pipe __
Pipe __ connects to pipe __

301

The Horizontal Line

In a rare ten minute coffee break, Detective
Hartland was recounting a story to Officer Barlow.

"When I was on leave in the USA one year I was
asked to observe a case. This was around, oh, 35
years ago now. It was very interesting. There was
great concern that Russian spies had infiltrated
an American site and sabotaged their equipment,"
recounted Hartland.

"Yes, we don't get too much of that sort of stuff
now that the Cold War is over," said Barlow.

Hartland continued. "Indeed, for the best of
course. I was one of a team investigating the case.
We were trying to determine whether it was a case
of espionage or whether it was just an unfortunate
mistake."

"And...?"

"Well, we couldn't really see any foul play and it
was widely suspected that it was just a mistake.
We didn't have a great deal to go on anyway.
Unfortunately, that one mistake cost $18 million."

"Jeez! I bet that stung the tax payers' pockets."
Barlow stood up to get another cup of coffee from
the percolator.

"Too right," said Hartland, "and the funniest
thing was that the mistake was caused by a short,
horizontal line!"

Barlow looked back at the Detective in
puzzlement. "A what?" he asked.

"A short, horizontal line. Why, I don't think you

need to be a great detective to work it out. There aren't too many things that are so expensive that they cost that much money to rebuild in their entirety. This certainly was an expensive job because the parts had to be made so precisely."

"Ah, so this was advanced tecchie stuff, then. Right, well I think I might have an idea of what you're on about now."

"Told you it wasn't difficult," said Hartland as he finished his coffee.

Do you know the actual event that the Detective is referring to?

Clues to ten of the longest words that we
managed to find :

1	Old age for a teeny-bopper
2	Life annuity scheme
3	Kind of fossil resin
4	Go into again
5	£10 or $10
6	Storm, sudden outburst
7	Animal's foot
8	A little laugh
9	Of the earth
10	One who answers back

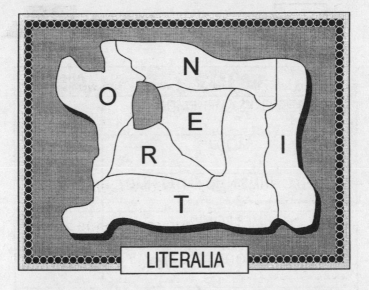

LITERALIA

Other words of five letters or more (find up to another 20) :

305

WHO?	GUESSES
BZSZOTKS CDRHFMDQ	**12**
RBQDV	**10**
SGQDD ONHMS NMD ENTQ NMD...	**8**
JHMFR BQNVM	**6**
FQDDJ	**4**
DTQDJZ	**2**

WHAT?	GUESSES
DHFGSX-DHFGS	**12**
PTHDS ZMC KNTC	**10**
GZLLDQR	**8**
VAVAVVAVAVAV	**6**
RSDHMVZX	**4**
KHADQZBD TRDC HS	**2**

WHERE?	GUESSES
QNXZK UDMTD	12
SNTQHRS ZSSQZBSHNM	10
DEEHFHDR	8
SVN ONHMS RHW LHKKHNM UHRHSNQR	6
CDZSG LZRJR	4
EQDMBG VZW VNQJR	2

WHEN?	GUESSES
SNLZGZVJ	12
SZQHP ZYHY	10
OZSQHNS	8
NHK ROHKK	6
JTVZHS	4
RZCCZL GTRRDHM	2

For each of the statements below, put your guesstimated answer in the appropriate box on the opposite page.

A   How many bank holidays does Germany have each year?

B   How many Wimbledon titles did Billie Jean King win?

C   How many theses did Luther nail to the door of the Wittenberg Church?

D   How many gallons of oil fit into a standard oil barrel?

E   How many centuries made up one legion in the Roman army?

F   How many feet high does the Statue of Liberty stand?

G   What is the life expectancy of an average Japanese male?

H   How many millions of copies of the *Los Angeles Times* are circulated each week?

J   How many 1000s of words must the title role actor in *Hamlet* speak each performance?

K   How many million books are there in the Library of Congress?

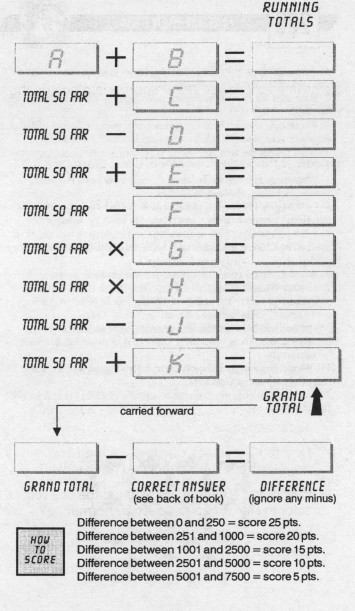

RUNNING TOTALS

A	+	B	=	
TOTAL SO FAR	+	C	=	
TOTAL SO FAR	−	D	=	
TOTAL SO FAR	+	E	=	
TOTAL SO FAR	−	F	=	
TOTAL SO FAR	×	G	=	
TOTAL SO FAR	×	H	=	
TOTAL SO FAR	−	J	=	
TOTAL SO FAR	+	K	=	

GRAND TOTAL

carried forward

| | − | | = | |
| GRAND TOTAL | | CORRECT ANSWER (see back of book) | | DIFFERENCE (ignore any minus) |

HOW TO SCORE

Difference between 0 and 250 = score 25 pts.
Difference between 251 and 1000 = score 20 pts.
Difference between 1001 and 2500 = score 15 pts.
Difference between 2501 and 5000 = score 10 pts.
Difference between 5001 and 7500 = score 5 pts.

1) Whose tomb in St Paul's Cathedral, London, bears the inscription "If you seek his monument, look around"?

2) How does the title of the French newspaper *Le Monde* translate into English?

3) Which bay, situated between Spain and France, is the site of famous ferocious seas and high tides, as detailed in a traditional song?

4) What fell for the first, and so far only, time in the Sahara Desert in 1979?

5) What name is given to flag designs such as those of Belgium, France, Germany, Holland and Italy?

6) On 7 March 1979 which planet was found to have rings like those of Saturn and Uranus from pictures relayed to Earth by *Voyager I*?

7) What yellow ingredient of fireworks and explosives was drunk in solution by Chinese emperors who believed it held the secret of long life?

8) Which is the odd one out – cone, rhombus, cuboid, pyramid, dodecahedron, sphere?

9) Called "the hall of the slain", in which place in Norse mythology could heroes' souls rest and eat with their chief, Odin?

10) In the 1960 US Presidential campaign, with which shifty occupation was Nixon mockingly connected in an anti-slogan used by his opponents?

11) What flavouring is common to the following drinks – curacao, chartreuse, Southern Comfort?

12) Who is seen clinging from the hands of a clock in his classic 1923 film *Safety Last*?

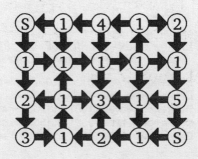

LAP 28

There are no time limits on this lap.

To score each puzzle, refer to the summary on pages 269–270. The maximum scores available are shown below.

	MAX.	SCORE
QUIZWORD	25	
REBUS CHALLENGE	30	
SAFE CRACKER	20	
LOGIC PROBLEM	20	
IN THE PIPELINE	20	
CRIME STORY	25	
WORD ISLAND	30	
MISSING LINKS	30	
NUMEROLOGY	25	
MAGNIFICENT MAZE	25	
TOTAL (max. 250)		

TARGET TO BEAT – 110 points

QUIZWORD

ACROSS

8 Where would milk be turned into butter and cheese products? (8)

9 What tube in the human body carries urine from the kidney to the bladder? (6)

10 What relation is your mother's husband's daughter to you if your mother's husband is not your father? (4-6)

11 In chemistry, if blue litmus paper is turned red, what does this indicate the presence of? (4)

12 In mathematics, what type of fraction has a numerator whose value is less than that of its denominator? (6)

14 Which word can be made from the letters "TORCH ICE"? (8)

15 What is a group of four performing musicians called? (7)

17 Which neurological disorder, which affects the ability to express ideas

312

or name objects, was the subject of Sigmund Freud's first published work? (7)

20 What type of photograph is made using interference of laser light on the film to show a 3-D image? (8)

22 Which famous make of British motorcycle won the Isle of Man TT races many times in the 1940s and 50s? (6)

24 What bird is the national emblem of New Zealand? (4)

25 What European and Asian amphibian gave rise, in part, to the word "gerrymander"? (10)

27 What word describes those people who are your relatives by marriage only? (2-4)

28 What is the name of the poisonous alkaline substance found in deadly nightshade? (8)

DOWN

1 On the Moon the largest of these is "Bailly" at 180 miles wide. What type of feature is it? (6)

2 Which fish, which has an average lifespan of 30 years, has breeds including koi, leather, mirror and scale? (4)

3 Which word describes animals whose ancestors are well documented and of the same breed? (8)

4 What type of story has various fiction subgenres including detective, romantic suspense and the adventure story? (7)

5 What term describes the instructions to candidates given on the front of an examination paper? (6)

6 What leisurely form of transport involves a covered seat for one being carried on two poles? (5-5)

7 Which disease is caused by a lack of vitamin B1? (8)

13 What is a regularly produced publication containing details of new scientific research? (10)

16 What name did Thomas More give to the inhabitants of his fictional state of perfection in a 1516 book? (8)

18 What is the name of the lighter shadow, around the cone of total darkness of lunar eclipses, caused by the Earth blocking the Sun's rays? (8)

19 What adjective describes alloys which include mercury? (7)

21 If a zigzag line is seen on an electric circuit to represent an electrical component, what does that component do to the flow of current? (6)

23 Of what are there five on the Earth's surface, the Pacific being the largest? (6)

26 What is the back of the neck called? (4)

1

FATAL

_ _ _ _ _   _ _ _ _ _ _ _ _ _ _

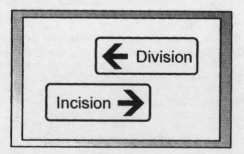

COMMERCIAL

2

_ _ _ _ _ _ _ _ _ _   _ _ _ _ _

3

← Division

Incision →

_ _ _ _   _ _ _ _   _ _ _ _

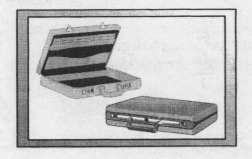

---- --- ---- ----

--- ---- --- -----

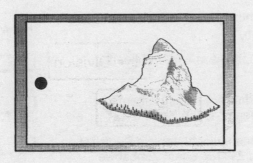

----- ----- -----

Blacken out those segments on the right-hand page that are letter coded to the FALSE statements. This will form a correct mathematical sum.

True False

A	SWAPO stands for South West Africa People's Organisation	☐ ☐
B	In architecture, a cupola is a round inlet into a church wall	☐ ☐
C	Tomas de Torquemada founded the Ku-Klux Klan	☐ ☐
D	The capital of South Korea is Seoul	☐ ☐
E	Shekels are the unit of currency in Israel	☐ ☐
F	J. R. R. Tolkien's initials stood for John Ronald Reuel	☐ ☐
G	The musical term doloroso means happily	☐ ☐
H	Ochlophobia is a fear of hearing	☐ ☐
J	The SI unit of measurement for wavelength is the Hertz (Hz)	☐ ☐
K	The International Vehicle Registration letters ZW represent Zimbabwe	☐ ☐

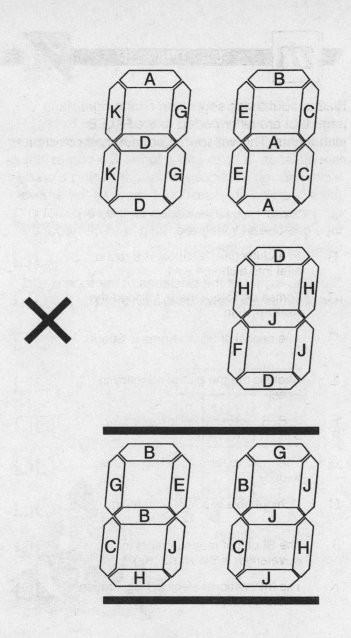

In the top-rating game show *Pick a Box*, contestants are invited to pick one of 25 boxes, although only 5 contain a card. On each card there is a question, a prize and a forfeit. If a contestant is lucky enough to choose a box containing a card, (s)he is asked the question. If they get the answer right they get the prize stated on the card, but if they get it wrong they are obliged to carry out the forfeit stated on the card.

Can you work out the positions of each card and what forfeits and rewards are on them?

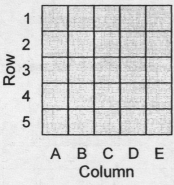

CLUES

1. Every row, column and both main diagonals all contain exactly one card.

2. The $10,000 prize is somewhere in column B.

3. The card in column E contains details of a forfeit where the contestant promptly receives a custard pie!

4. Contestants wanting the $2,000 prize also run the risk of having to donate $100 to charity if they get the question wrong.

5. The card in Row 2 says "Forfeit – you must walk the host's dogs every day for a week!"

6. The card in Row 1 has the jackpot prize of $25,000. It is not in Column A.

7. There is a prize in box 4C but not in 1E.

8. The $5,000 prize doesn't carry the custard pie forfeit nor the one where the contestant has to endure being driven round a stock car racing circuit at high speed.

9. Column A doesn't contain the forfeit asking the contestant to take part in a wrestling competition.

STARTING HINTS

a. Use clues 1, 2, 6 and 7 to deduce the whereabouts of the $25,000 jackpot prize.

b. Now consider clue 1 very carefully.

NOTE – The five prizes are : $1,000; $2,000; $5,000; $10,000;

Card positions			
Row	Column	Forfeit	Prize
1			
2			
3			
4			
5			

IN THE PIPELINE

Your task is to associate the classic films below with the actors that appeared in them.

1. *Crazy People*
2. *Return of the Jedi*
3. *Bad Day at Black Rock*
4. *A Passage to India*
5. *The Shootist*
6. *The Poseidon Adventure*
7. *Hannah and Her Sisters*
8. *Arthur*
9. *Much Ado About Nothing*
10. *The Lady Killers*
11. *Bridge on the River Kwai*
12. *It's a Mad Mad Mad Mad World*
13. *Beau Geste*
14. *Sleeper*
15. *Husbands and Wives*
16. *The Naked Gun*
17. *Anatomy of a Murder*
18. *How the West was Won*
19. *Father of the Bride*
20. *Nuts*

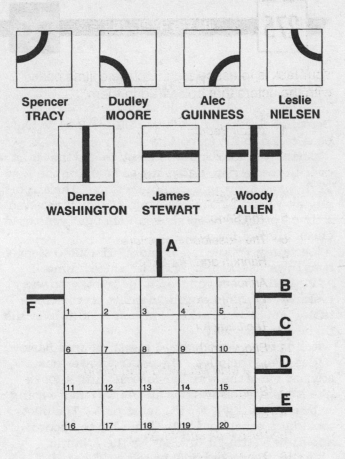

Spencer
TRACY

Dudley
MOORE

Alec
GUINNESS

Leslie
NIELSEN

Denzel
WASHINGTON

James
STEWART

Woody
ALLEN

Your answer :
Pipe __ connects to pipe __
Pipe __ connects to pipe __
Pipe __ connects to pipe __

321

The Phoney Pilot

Detective Hartland and Police Officer Barlow had been called to the airport.

"Thank you for coming, Detective. It's that pilot over in the corner. He's going to be flying the New York plane in around an hour's time." The airport manager was slightly sweating. "I've just received a tip-off over the telephone so I thought you could check him out for me."

"Certainly. Follow me, Barlow." Hartland stepped over towards the pilot and introduced himself.

"Pleased to meet you," said the pilot, who was looking over a fold-out flight chart on the coffee table. "I'm Steven Parker. I'm just looking over the flight plan for today."

"Going to be a good trip, I hope," offered Barlow.

"Yes," said the pilot, "the control tower has advised me of the weather forecast and it looks like it's almost clear skies all the way so it's going to be a direct flight for the most part." The pilot took out a pencil and ruler from his top pocket and drew a straight line across the Atlantic.

"Is that the route you'll be taking?" asked Hartland.

"Well, not exactly, but that's our planned flight path. Of course, it's mainly down to computerised navigation and some radio contact nowadays but it helps to get an idea of the visual landmarks, just for my own peace of mind. Of course, the co-pilot helps also."

"So how long have you been a pilot, sir?" asked Barlow.

"Around 12 years now. Bit of an old hand at these transatlantic flights. I've worked for all the major companies including British Airways and American Airlines." The pilot took a sip of his coffee. "Well, I'm afraid I have to go, gentlemen, because we have to do numerous pre-flight checks before we take off. Don't want to take any risks now, do we!" he chortled.

"I'm afraid that won't be necessary, Mr Parker, because you'll be answering some questions back at the police station."

Can you spot what had particularly aroused Detective Hartland's suspicions about the "pilot"?

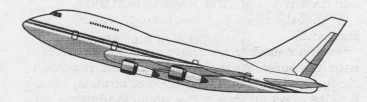

Clues to ten of the longest words that we
managed to find :

1	Tie-breaker
2	Turned back, yielded again
3	Laughed at, mocked
4	A judicial decision
5	Banished
6	A French posterior?
7	Danced in a Scottish way?
8	The murder of a god
9	Looked at lecherously
10	Spooky, weird

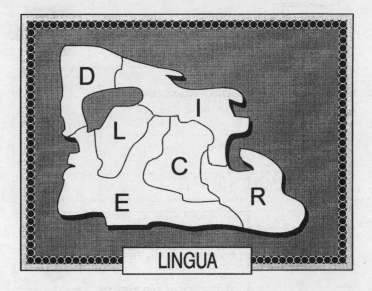

LINGUA

Other words of five letters or more (find up to
another 20) :

WHO?	GUESSES
RBQHAAKDQ	12
ZBSNQ	10
MZLD BGZMFD	8
FKNAD SGDZSQD	6
GZSGZVZX	4
AZQC NE ZUNM	2

WHAT?	GUESSES
SDM NM LNGR' RBZKD	12
D.F. AQHKKHZMS NQ QNRD	10
FQZOGHSD	8
ADRS EQHDMC?	6
RSZQ NE ZEQHBZ	4
BZQZS	2

WHERE?	GUESSES
MDV EQNMS	12
LDLNQHZK ENTMSZHM	10
NM SGD LZKK	8
RHW GTMCQDC QNNLR	6
QNXZK RSZMCZQC EKHDR	4
SGD FTZQC BGZMFDR SGDQD	2

WHEN?	GUESSES
DZQK VZQQDM	12
IZBJ QTAX	10
MNUDLADQ MHMDSDDM RHWSX-SGQDD	8
BNMROHQZBX?	6
RSZSD UHRHS SN CZKKZR	4
KDD GZQUDX NRVZKC	2

For each of the statements below, put your guesstimated answer in the appropriate box on the opposite page.

A   How many sides does an icosahedron have?

B   How many pedals does a standard musical harp have?

C   How many twins appear in Shakespeare's *A Comedy of Errors*?

D   How many popes have been assassinated?

E   How many gold medals did Mark Spitz win in the 1968/72 Olympics?

F   How many stomachs do cattle have?

G   A marathon is 26 miles long plus another how many yards?

H   How many locks does the Panama Canal have?

J   How many million passengers use Chicago's O'Hare International Airport per annum?

K   How many chromosomes does a human being have?

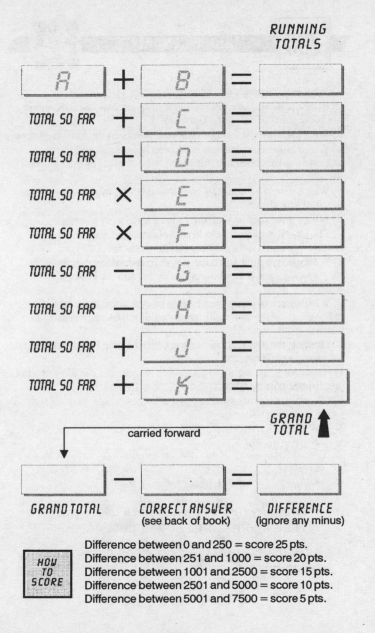

RUNNING
TOTALS

A + B =

TOTAL SO FAR + C =

TOTAL SO FAR + D =

TOTAL SO FAR × E =

TOTAL SO FAR × F =

TOTAL SO FAR − G =

TOTAL SO FAR − H =

TOTAL SO FAR + J =

TOTAL SO FAR + K =

GRAND
TOTAL

carried forward

GRAND TOTAL − CORRECT ANSWER = DIFFERENCE
(see back of book)   (ignore any minus)

HOW
TO
SCORE

Difference between 0 and 250 = score 25 pts.
Difference between 251 and 1000 = score 20 pts.
Difference between 1001 and 2500 = score 15 pts.
Difference between 2501 and 5000 = score 10 pts.
Difference between 5001 and 7500 = score 5 pts.

1) What is the world's widest river?

2) In whose honour are festivals held in Glyndebourne, UK and in his home town of Salzburg, Germany?

3) What are the most famous antipodal points on the Earth's surface?

4) Which American state has the lowest population and the most extreme male/female ratio due to the large number of men that work there?

5) Which part of an animal's body could be described as prehensile if it was especially versatile?

6) Which three chemical elements are named after planets?

7) The Greek mathematician Euclid claimed there were only five "regular" solids – what is so regular about them?

8) Which horrid mythical creatures were encountered by Jason and his Argonauts and looked like vultures but had the heads of old women?

9) Which piece of equipment is used by occultists to receive messages from the spirits, its name deriving from the French and German words for "Yes"?

10) What is the political connection between Mondale, Rockefeller, Johnson, Ford, Bush, and Quale?

11) In which game are up to six people involved in the investigation into the death of Dr Black?

12) How many events are there in the women's equivalent of the men's decathlon?

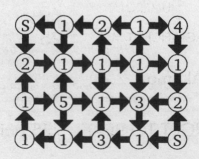

LAP 29

There are no time limits on this lap.

To score each puzzle, refer to the summary on pages 269–270. The maximum scores available are shown below.

	MAX.	SCORE
QUIZWORD	25	
REBUS CHALLENGE	30	
SAFE CRACKER	20	
LOGIC PROBLEM	20	
IN THE PIPELINE	20	
CRIME STORY	25	
WORD ISLAND	30	
MISSING LINKS	30	
NUMEROLOGY	25	
MAGNIFICENT MAZE	25	
TOTAL (max. 250)		

TARGET TO BEAT – 125 points

ACROSS

8 What flower is a variation of the buttercup, with smaller petals? (8)

9 What word, also used as a suffix, describes an irrational fear of a particular situation, place or object? (6)

10 What is the common name for the hyoid bone at the front of the neck, so called because of a legend in Genesis, Chapter 3? (5,5)

11 What name is given a person who comes from regions of northern Finland, Norway or Sweden? (4)

12 An emergency or state of panic (6)

14 What is the practice of giving employment to those related to you, rather than on the basis of individual merit? (8)

15 Which form of government was employed in Italy in 1922–1943? (7)

17 What classical architectural features rest on a base and are surmounted by capitals? (7)

332

20 What word, also meaning "concerning the head", is the name of an index concerned with various head measurements? (8)

22 Which Egyptian city was a capital of ancient Egypt and is the site of present-day Luxor and Al-Karnak? (6)

24 In astronomy, what is a large body of gases, held together by gravity, that emits radiations sometimes including visible light? (4)

25 This word means to shorten (10)

27 What alloy is primarily made from copper and tin? (6)

28 What word connects a county of New York City, a borough of London, and the main Confederate capital during the American Civil War? (8)

DOWN

1 Anyone involved in the buying and selling of goods, in particular those who use bartering (6)

2 Which of the three sporting activities in a triathlon do contestants perform first? (4)

3 Which by-product of sugar, also called treacle, was taxed in the USA by the British Parliament in the 18th Century? (8)

4 What term describes a soldier's pay, or the payment received by a parish minister in Scotland? (7)

5 The maintenance of a building or the costs involved (6)

6 Which salad vegetable comes from the second largest of the Dodecanese Islands? (3,7)

7 In music, the _____ normal is a standard set in the 1887 Vienna Conference to fix the pitch of the A above middle C (8)

13 Which powder, prepared from toluene, is 550 times sweeter than sugar in its purest state? (10)

16 Which part of a camera is a hole variable in size to alter the amount of light that falls onto the film? (8)

18 What word means "to overstretch" and "the extent of involvement of an organisation with the surrounding population"? (8)

19 What punctured five of the *Titanic*'s sixteen waterproof compartments, causing it to sink, on April 14, 1912? (7)

21 St. Peter is closely associated with the Bible story of the _____ and fishes (6)

23 What word, derived from Latin, means "to still be standing or existing"? (6)

26 What is a part of a verse consisting of an unstressed syllable followed by a stressed one? (4)

1

GRAVITY
↑

_ _ _ _ _ _   _ _   _ _ _ _ _ _ _

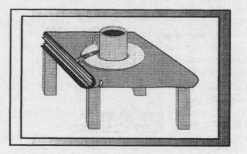 2

_ _ _ _ _ _   _ _ _ _ _   _ _ _ _

3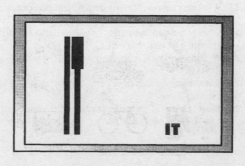

IT

_ _ _   _ _ _ _   _ _ _
_ _ _ _ _   _ _   _ _

_ _ _ _ _ _ _ _   _ _ _ _ _

UNITED KINGDOM
GREECE
ITALY
AUSTRALIA
USA
CHINA
BRAZIL
GERMANY
NEW ZEALAND

3 nautical miles

_ _ _   _ _ _ _ _ _
_ _   _ _ _ _ _ _ _

_ _ _ _   _ _ _   _ _ _

Blacken out those segments on the right-hand page that are letter coded to the FALSE statements. This will form a correct mathematical sum.

True False

A   The Wright Brothers made the first powered flight at Kitty Hawk, NC ☐ ☐

B   In a suit of armour, the gorget protects the upper arm ☐ ☐

C   *Yesterday* was the theme song for the film *On Her Majesty's Secret Service* ☐ ☐

D   Khartoum is the capital city of the Sudan ☐ ☐

E   The Aswan High Dam is situated on the River Volga ☐ ☐

F   Otis invented the lift in 1752 ☐ ☐

G   Ernest Hemingway never won the Nobel Prize for literature ☐ ☐

H   Androphobia is a fear of electronic gadgets ☐ ☐

J   In physics, the becquerel is a measure of radioactivity ☐ ☐

K   Sagittarius is the zodiac sign of "the archer" ☐ ☐

336

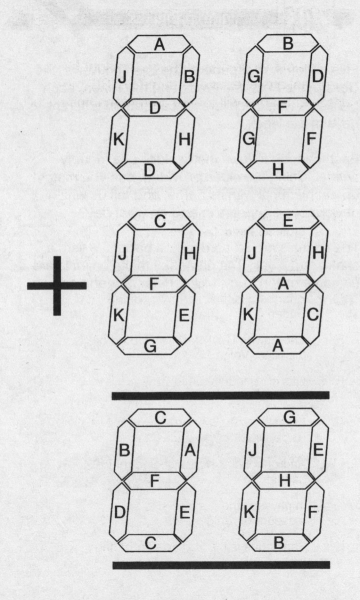

337

Five national newspapers (the *Evening News*, the
Gossip, the *Post*, the *Press* and the *Times*) each
publish a weekly children's cartoon on different
days of the week.

Each cartoon follows the exploits of a friendly
animal. Using the clues provided, can you match
up each animal with its name, and tell us which
newspaper it appears in and on what day?

The animals are an aardvark, a badger, a fish, a
snake and a yak. The names of these animals are
(in some order) Lucy, Millie, Peter, Simone and
Trevor.

CLUES

1. Lucy the Snake appears two days before the *Press* runs its cartoon which features the exploits of Millie.

2. Trevor appears on Wednesdays.

3. The *Evening News* runs its children's cartoon on Fridays without fail, but it is not the paper that has Simone the Fish.

4. The aardvark appears in the *Gossip*, which doesn't have cartoons on Mondays.

5. The *Post* doesn't have cartoons on Mondays either.

6. Peter is not a yak.

STARTING HINTS

a. Bearing in mind clue 2, take a close look at clue 1. You should be able to deduce the publication days for Lucy and Millie straight away.

b. The next bit is more tricky. One possibility is to examine each animal, determine which names are possible, and also which days they could possibly come out on. You should be able to deduce the days when the aardvark and fish are printed.

NOTE – The papers only come out on Mondays through Fridays, there being no weekend editions.

Animal	Name	Paper	Day
Aardvark			
Badger			
Fish			
Snake			
Yak			

Your task is to connect the book titles below with their female authors (right).

1 *Jamaica Inn*

2 *Mansfield Park*

3 *Jane Eyre*

4 *Hollywood Wives*

5 *Whose Body?*

6 *The Five Red Herrings*

7 *The ABC Murders*

8 *The Nine Tailors*

9 *Sense and Sensibility*

10 *N or M?*

11 *A Woman of Substance*

12 *Lord Peter Views the Body*

13 *Emma*

14 *Sparkling Cyanide*

15 *Strong Poison*

16 *4.50 from Paddington*

17 *To Be the Best*

18 *The Birds*

19 *The Professor*

20 *The Pale Horse*

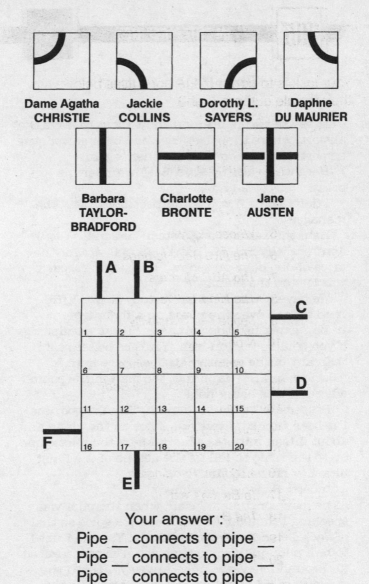

Dame Agatha CHRISTIE

Jackie COLLINS

Dorothy L. SAYERS

Daphne DU MAURIER

Barbara TAYLOR-BRADFORD

Charlotte BRONTE

Jane AUSTEN

Your answer :

Pipe __ connects to pipe __

Pipe __ connects to pipe __

Pipe __ connects to pipe __

The False Alarm

Just as the two policemen were about to leave the airport, where their last case had been solved, the airport manager confronted them again.

"Here we go again," said Barlow under his breath.

"I don't know if you could possibly..." said the manager.

"Help you again?" suggested Hartland. "Yes, I don't see why not. We have a special two-for-the-price-of-one offer on today." Hartland's sarcasm was lost on the manager.

"We have a man held in Custody Room 3. He tried to take over the plane on a flight from India," explained the manager. "I was wondering if you could question him. You'd be better at it than any of the security staff we have here."

Barlow and Hartland met the man in the room where he was being held.

"Policemen?" asked the man. "Thank goodness. I've been framed, I tell you. I got on the plane and about fifteen minutes after take-off the pilot came on to the radio to tell us the details of the flight, like they normally do."

"Indeed. So what happened?"

The man continued. "Well, when the pilot was speaking I thought I recognised his voice as that of Jack Delaney, a friend of mine. You see I used to be a pilot quite some time ago. I've been retired for around five years now. Anyway, I asked the stewardess if I could go and meet him. She said

'Yes', so I got up out of my seat and went up to the pilots' cabin, knocked on the door and said hello. At that moment, these two security goons pounced on me and within seconds I was dragged off to the back of the plane to be held there for the rest of the journey. I don't understand it."

At that moment the airport manager entered the room. "How are the investigations going, Detective?"

Hartland was puzzled. "Is it usual to have security guards aboard a plane?"

"No," said the manager, "but today's trip had a few private security guards because there were a couple of Indian film celebrities on that flight."

"Well," concluded the Detective, "I think they should be better trained. This man you are holding has done nothing wrong and this whole situation is an unfortunate mistake on the part of the security guards. They should listen more carefully."

Can you work out what the man had done unintentionally to alarm the guards so much?

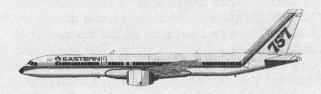

Clues to ten of the longest words that we managed to find :

1	*Eastern art of knot-tying*
2	*Colloquial for 'mater'*
3	*Containing more milk?*
4	*Photographic device*
5	*School of rote learning?*
6	*A debt*
7	*More jovial*
8	*Genus of plants*
9	*Transporter of disease/virus*
10	*Caribbean percussion instrument*

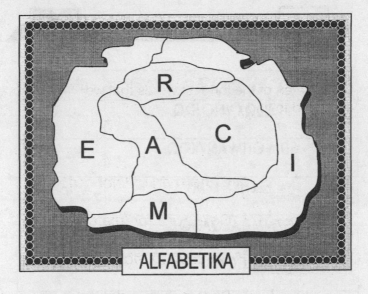

ALFABETIKA

Other words of five letters or more (find up to another 20) :

WHO?	GUESSES
PTZQQX VNQJDQ	12
SDM OHM ANVKDQ	10
EZLHKX LZM	8
GZMMZ AZQADQZ	6
ADCQNBJ	4
OQDGHRSNQHB	2

WHAT?	GUESSES
VVH NARDQUZSHNM ONRS	12
DHFGSDDM DHFGSX-MHMD DWGHAHSHNM	10
SGQDD GTMCQDC LDSQDR	8
BGZLO CD LZQR	6
CDRHFMDQ FTRSZUD...	4
EQDMBG KZMCLZQJ	2

WHERE?	GUESSES
QNXZK QDRHCDMBD	12
YHFFTQZS	10
ENTQ NQ EHUD RHCDR	8
BGDNOR	6
SNLA	4
DFXOS	2

WHEN?	GUESSES
GZVJR	12
EZM BKTA	10
ONHMCDWSDQ	8
RDBQDSZQX	6
RGQDCCDC	4
NKHUDQ MNQSG	2

347

NUMEROLOGY

For each of the statements below, put your guesstimated answer in the appropriate box on the opposite page.

A At what age does a Jewish man celebrate his Bar Mitzvah?

B How many provinces does Canada have?

C What number does L represent in Roman numerals?

D How many books are there in the New Testament?

E How many feet long was Bob Beamon's famous world record long jump?

F How many million dollars did Bill Cosby earn in 1992–3?

G How many keys are on a standard piano keyboard?

H How many items of mail does the average person in Switzerland receive per annum?

J On average, a murder in the USA takes place every how many minutes?

K How many inches apart are the rails on a Standard Gauge railway?

| A | × | B | = | |

| TOTAL SO FAR | − | C | = | |

| TOTAL SO FAR | − | D | = | |

| TOTAL SO FAR | + | E | = | |

| TOTAL SO FAR | − | F | = | |

| TOTAL SO FAR | × | G | = | |

| TOTAL SO FAR | − | H | = | |

| TOTAL SO FAR | − | J | = | |

| TOTAL SO FAR | + | K | = | |

GRAND
TOTAL ▲

carried forward

| | − | | = | |

GRAND TOTAL   CORRECT ANSWER   DIFFERENCE
               (see back of book)   (ignore any minus)

HOW TO SCORE

Difference between 0 and 250 = score 25 pts.
Difference between 251 and 1000 = score 20 pts.
Difference between 1001 and 2500 = score 15 pts.
Difference between 2501 and 5000 = score 10 pts.
Difference between 5001 and 7500 = score 5 pts.

1) Which film character uses the cover of working for the company Universal Import and Export?

2) Which of the great lakes is completely contained within the United States?

3) What is the world's second largest country?

4) Lord Tennyson's poem *The Charge of the Light Brigade* describes how 600 men on horseback rode "into the valley of Death". This was the Battle of Balaklava, during which war?

5) For what sporting purpose are ostriches, horses and camels used?

6) What general chemical term is applied to a substance created using large chains of much smaller molecules?

7) The AB blood group is called the "receive-all group" because people with it can take blood from any other group. Which group is the "donate-all" group?

8) On what fortune-telling objects would you find cups, pentacles, swords and wands in the Minor Arcana?

9) Which Italian designer's clothes were so popular, possibly due to his style of suit being worn by Richard Gere in the film *American Gigolo*, that he began designing for women as well?

10) Which game, a craze during the 1920s in the USA, requires 152 tiles divided up into 36 bamboos, 36 circles, 36 characters, 12 dragons, 16 winds, 8 jokers, and 8 flowers?

11) Which is the longest track event to use starting blocks?

12) If a chequered flag finishes a race and a yellow flag indicates "no overtaking", what does a black flag indicate?

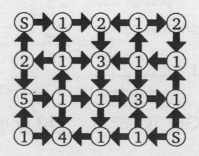

There are no time limits on this lap.

To score each puzzle, refer to the summary on pages 269–270. The maximum scores available are shown below.

	MAX.	SCORE
QUIZWORD	25	
REBUS CHALLENGE	30	
SAFE CRACKER	20	
LOGIC PROBLEM	20	
IN THE PIPELINE	20	
CRIME STORY	25	
WORD ISLAND	30	
MISSING LINKS	30	
NUMEROLOGY	25	
MAGNIFICENT MAZE	25	
TOTAL (max. 250)		

TARGET TO BEAT – 140 points

ACROSS

8 For what physical phenomenon did Sir Isaac Newton describe three laws that are still fundamental to physics today? (6)

9 Which fictitious city did the Spanish conquerors of America search for in the pursuit of its fabled golden riches? (2,6)

10 What is the simplest form of a hydraulic turbine called, as first described by the Roman architect Pollio in the 1st Century BC? (10)

11 What type of blood vessel carries deoxygenated blood from the capillaries back to the heart? (4)

12 What occurs when the sea is returning towards its lowest level? (3,4)

14 What cake is made from a long choux pastry case filled with whipped cream and topped with icing? (6)

15 This could describe the inhabitants of the land of Lilliput, in Jonathan Swift's book *Gulliver's Travels* (7)

17 In which sport is the Americas' Cup contested for? (7)

20 What title is given to the clergyman of a parish or congregation to which tithes are not payable? (6)

22 What variation of the fox-trot takes its name from the action of moving the feet with every beat of the music? (3-4)

24 In architecture, what term describes the supports of an arch, bridge or similar spanning structure? (4)

25 What practice, most often associated with the Roman Catholic church, is the act of granting penance based upon *John*, Chapter 20? (10)

27 In computing, what word describes those workers who will actually operate the finished program? (3,5)

28 Name a relative of the violin (6)

DOWN

1 Esau sold his birthright to Jacob for a bowlful of what? (6)

2 A varied assortment (5,3)

3 What crystals form around dust particles and always grow in a pattern with three lines of symmetry? (4)

4 What name is given to the official presiding over a match in sports such as lacrosse, basketball, tennis and soccer? (7)

5 Which term means "to add cheaper ingredients to make the commodity more impure with the aim of increasing profits"? (10)

6 Name the loose, rounded fragments of rock often used as a finishing material for driveways and roofs? (6)

7 Which of the four basic mathematical operations is used when computing the "sum" of some numbers? (8)

13 What are the textual and/or graphical devices used in computer programs to allow the user to tell the program what actions to perform? (10)

16 What are the people of ancient eastern and southern Spain called? (8)

18 What geometrical coordinate gives the North or South location of a place relative to the equator? (8)

19 This word means "to own" (7)

21 In physics, what type of force is induced when a turning motion results even though the resultant force may be in equilibrium? (6)

23 What type of dog has varieties including the standard, miniature and toy? (6)

26 On which side is something if it can be described as "sinister"? (4)

_ _ _ _ _ _   _ _ _ _   _ _ _ _ _

EDGEAWORDWAYS

_ _ _ _ _ _   _ _   _ _ _ _ _ _ _ _

_ _ _   _ _ _   _ _ _ _ _ _

PERSIAN
SIAMESE
TURKISH
TORTOISE SHELL
BIRMAN
ABYSSINIAN

◀ 4

---- ----

▶ 5

--------- -------

◀ 6

---- ------- ----

Blacken out those segments on the right-hand page that are letter coded to the FALSE statements. This will form a correct mathematical sum.

True False

A   The national airline of Portugal is VARIG. ☐ ☐

B   Nathuran Godse shot Mohandas K. Ghandi in 1948 ☐ ☐

C   A jeroboam of champagne holds a volume equivalent to 16 wine bottles ☐ ☐

D   The old name for Tungsten is Wolfram ☐ ☐

E   The cities in Dickens's *A Tale of Two Cities* are London and Berlin ☐ ☐

F   Gutenberg invented moveable type in 1450 ☐ ☐

G   Paris was the first city to host the modern Olympic games twice ☐ ☐

H   Phobos and Deimos are the two moons of Neptune ☐ ☐

J   The clavicle is the proper name for what is called the breastbone ☐ ☐

K   If you are born on August 28th, your sun sign is Taurus ☐ ☐

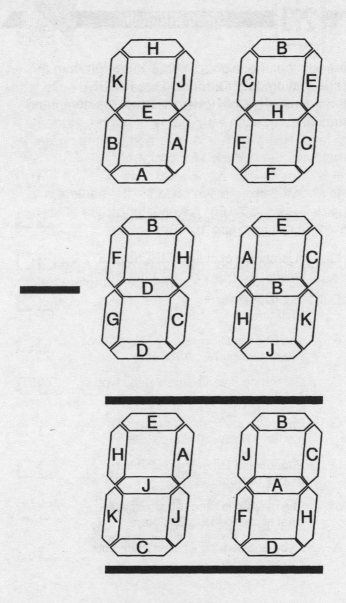

Alfredo the chef works at Your Kinda Pizza in the university town of Dunelm. There are five colleges there (Aidan's, Collingwood, Grey, Trevelyan and Van Mildert), each with plenty of hungry students to feed. However, he can't remember the orders that have been placed for tonight.

He knows there are five orders – the earliest is to be delivered at 7:15pm, with later orders at 8pm, 8:30pm, 9:15pm and 10:30pm.

Using the information he can remember (see clues) can you piece together the complete details of all five orders?

CLUES

1. "I remember that Martin's pizza (the exotically named Fuengerola) has to be delivered exactly 45 minutes later than the pepperoni heading for Aidan's."

2. "Oh yes, and the order for the pizza with anchovies was immediately after the Grey college order."

3. "I know Kay is in Trevelyan college because she's a regular customer. She wants a Hot & Spicy... or is it the Margherita?"

4. "The order to Collingwood needs to be there two hours before Ian wants his pizza. Actually, now I think about it, it might be a longer gap than that. I can't remember."

5. "I certainly know Heather wants her order for 8:30."

6. "Debbie's order isn't the 7:15 nor the 10:30. I know she never has the Hot & Spicy."

STARTING HINTS

a. Use clues 1, 4, 5 and 6 to work out who wants their pizzas at 7:15pm and 10:30pm.

b. Now use clues 1 and 3 to deduce the time at which the pepperoni pizza needs to be ordered.

c. From then on, it shouldn't be too difficult to deduce which student is from Collingwood college.

Name	College	Pizza	Time
Debbie			
Heather			
Ian			
Kay			
Martin			

Your task is to decide in which continents the mountains below are situated, though two of these are red herrings – for these, use the horizontal piece indicated (right).

1 Champlain

2 Everest

3 Kilimanjaro

4 Fujiyama

5 Erebus

6 Kirkpatrick

7 Stromboli

8 Mount of Olives

9 Logan

10 Popocatepetl

11 Matterhorn

12 Olympus

13 Parnassus

14 Townsend

15 Cotopaxi

16 Aconcagua

17 Sugar Loaf Mountain

18 Table Mountain

19 Titicaca

20 Cook

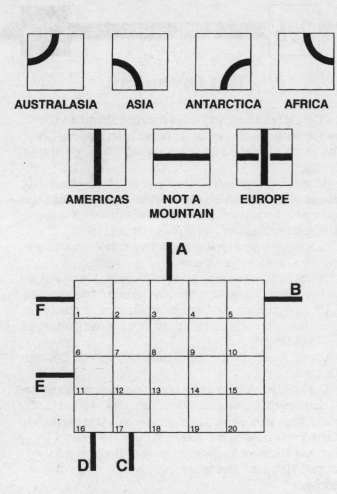

AUSTRALASIA ASIA ANTARCTICA AFRICA

AMERICAS NOT A MOUNTAIN EUROPE

Your answer :
Pipe __ connects to pipe __
Pipe __ connects to pipe __
Pipe __ connects to pipe __

The Great Fall

As Detective Hartland was driving towards the
police station, the radio buzzed into action. The
Detective returned the call signal. "Yes, go ahead,
Penny."

"Morning, Detective. Can you go to the building
site at Kensington Yard? Builders have found the
body of a young woman. No name yet but we're
still getting details," the radio crackled.

Hartland was there within five minutes. He was
met by the foreman there.

"Hello, sir, my name is Pete Norris. We've got a
rather nasty situation on our hands. The second
shift had just started work when one of the lads
discovered a body at the bottom of a long shaft in
the building."

"Could I see where this shaft is?" asked Detective
Hartland.

"Certainly." At that moment the foreman spotted
a man leaving the site. He called over to him. "Oi!
Geoff! Can you show this gentleman the same
thing you showed me earlier?" He turned to
address Hartland again. "Geoff will show you
round. He's the one working on that floor at the
moment."

The builder turned round and said "Follow me, if
you would." He led Hartland up the stairs to the
fourth floor of the building-to-be. "Quite a lot of
the work is unfinished so watch your step. Here
we are. I was here for the first shift this morning
and the situation was exactly like this. But if you

look here..." The builder went to open a nearby door and pointed downwards to indicate the gaping hole in the floor. "This shaft is going to be a lift but before that's installed we use it as a hatch for a pulley system. Near the end of my shift I was raising a few planks that I wanted to bring up to this floor when I noticed this body at the very bottom."

The Detective looked down the shaft and saw the body which the builders had covered in a blanket. "Nasty. What do you reckon happened?"

The builder thought for a moment. "Well, either she was suicidal or she was just being nosy and fell without realising there wasn't a floor on the other side of the door."

"Yes, those are possibilities, but I know it was murder and so do you!"

How did the Detective know this was a murder?

Clues to ten of the longest words that we managed to find :

1	Female higher being
2	Avoided
3	Hated to a great extent
4	The most strange
5	Hearty, but unhealthy, food
6	Secondary actor
7	Spotty
8	Plant, similar to grass
9	Added up, totalled
10	Ranked (as in tennis)

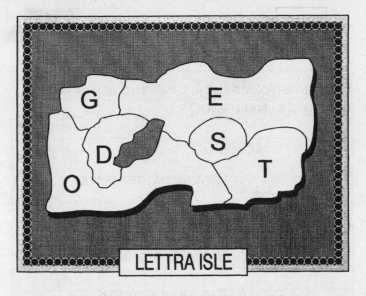

LETTRA ISLE

Other words of five letters or more (find up to another 20) :

WHO?	GUESSES
JNMHFRADQF	12
RKDDODQ	10
OZQZMNHC?	8
ZLDQHBZM	6
CHZMD JDZSNM	4
ZBSR/VQHSDR/CHQDBSR	2

WHAT?	GUESSES
QDLHMFSNM	12
HAL RDUDMSX-SVN	10
BZM AD DKDBSQHB	8
BZQQHZFD	6
SZATKZSHNM	4
PVDQSXTHNO	2

WHERE?	GUESSES
FQDZS EHQD	12
BZOHSNKHMD	10
SQDZSHDR	8
KZYHN	6
RDUDM GHKKR	4
BNKNRRDTL	2

WHEN?	GUESSES
KNMF CHRSZMBD VZKJ	12
SDKDOGNMD BZKK	10
MHMDSDDM-RHWSX-MHMD	8
SQZMPTHKKHSX	6
DZFKD	4
ZQLRSQNMF ZMC ZKCQHM	2

For each of the statements below, put your guesstimated answer in the appropriate box on the opposite page.

A How many dice are usually provided in a backgammon set?

B How many points does a field goal score in American football?

C How many billion people are there likely to be on Earth by the year 2025?

D How many minutes long can a solar eclipse last if viewed from the Earth's surface?

E How many hours long does Wagner's *Gotterdammerung* last?

F What is the maximum number of clubs a professional golfer can carry on a round?

G What percentage of Japan is covered by forest?

H How many Nobel Prizes has the United States won to date?

J How many million miles is it from the Earth to the Sun?

K What is the average life expectancy, in years, of a man from Sierra Leone?

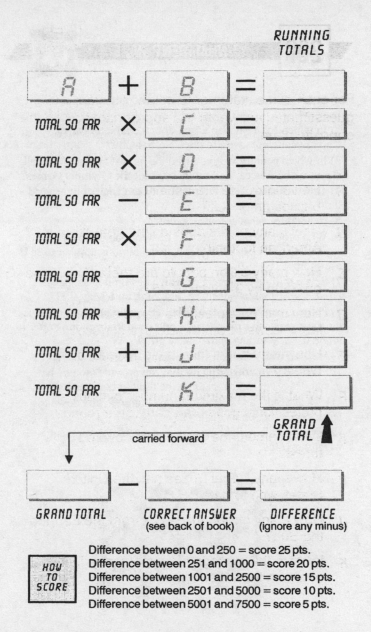

RUNNING TOTALS

A + B = ___

TOTAL SO FAR × C = ___

TOTAL SO FAR × D = ___

TOTAL SO FAR − E = ___

TOTAL SO FAR × F = ___

TOTAL SO FAR − G = ___

TOTAL SO FAR + H = ___

TOTAL SO FAR + J = ___

TOTAL SO FAR − K = ___

GRAND TOTAL ↑

carried forward

___ − ___ = ___

GRAND TOTAL | CORRECT ANSWER (see back of book) | DIFFERENCE (ignore any minus)

HOW TO SCORE

Difference between 0 and 250 = score 25 pts.
Difference between 251 and 1000 = score 20 pts.
Difference between 1001 and 2500 = score 15 pts.
Difference between 2501 and 5000 = score 10 pts.
Difference between 5001 and 7500 = score 5 pts.

1) In architecture, what term describes columns supporting a handrail?

2) In which John Bunyan novel does a character called Christian attempt to get to the Celestial City?

3) In which country will you find the largest covered football stadium, the Azteca, opened in 1968 for the Olympic Games?

4) To which side of the International Date Line does Madrid lie?

5) In heraldry, what colour is azure?

6) Who provides the connection between the discoverer of the expanding universe, a telescope, and a famous number used in astronomy?

7) Seven million cubic feet of which gas ignited as the *Hindenburg* airship was hit by lightning on 6 May, 1937?

8) Perhaps contrary to popular belief, which precious stone is the most expensive despite five other materials coming after it in the list of wedding anniversary gifts?

9) Medusa was a Gorgon – how many sisters did she have?

10) What does a polygraph do that can provide (somewhat inconclusive) evidence that may be used in court cases?

11) What drink can be graded from Orange Pekoe down to Dust, depending on its quality?

12) Which athletic field event uses a piece of equipment weighing 16lbs?

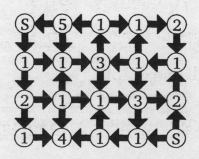

LAP 31

There are no time limits on this lap.

To score each puzzle, refer to the summary on pages 269–270. The maximum scores available are shown below.

	MAX.	SCORE
QUIZWORD	25	
REBUS CHALLENGE	30	
SAFE CRACKER	20	
LOGIC PROBLEM	20	
IN THE PIPELINE	20	
CRIME STORY	25	
WORD ISLAND	30	
MISSING LINKS	30	
NUMEROLOGY	25	
MAGNIFICENT MAZE	25	
TOTAL (max. 250)		

TARGET TO BEAT – 155 points

ACROSS

8 What musical term describes notes of given pitches and lengths sounding one after another to provide the "top line" of a score? (6)

9 Which animal derives its name from the Afrikaans for "earth pig"? (8)

10 Which legal term describes those rules that have been expressly enforced through legislation? (7-3)

11 Josip Broz _____, a former president of Yugoslavia, died in 1980 (4)

12 Of what are there types such as pressurised water, light water, boiling water and fast-breeder? (7)

14 What are the words that accompany the main tunes of songs called? (6)

15 Which part of the body is the most commonly pierced for cosmetic purposes? (7)

17 Which classic Activision/Atari computer game, recently re-released, invited the player to guide a character over rope swings and crocodiles? (7)

20 What is a person who practises water divining using a hazel stick called? (6)

22 What is the common name for herbs of the Ambrosia genus, noted for their small, green flowers on upright fronds? (7)

24 What was the name of the Pet Shop Boys' 1993 album, with its distinctive plastic orange CD box? (4)

25 What is the capital of Ethiopia? (5,5)

27 Which section of the Christian church takes this word of its name from the Greek word for "universal"? (8)

28 Which bird is famous for laying its eggs in the nests of other birds (although not all types do so)? (6)

DOWN

1 In mathematics, what is a line segment that has a length and a direction called? (6)

2 Which sport did the ancient Greeks call "harpaston", the Romans "harpastum" and the medieval Italians "calcio"? (8)

3 What medical term describes a sac filled with foreign matter (usually liquid)? (4)

4 What is the common name for the wild, surface-feeding duck from which the domestic duck has descended? (7)

5 Which metalwork technique uses a continuous supply of electric current to join two pieces of metal, most commonly steel? (3-7)

6 What Hindu principle, derived from Sanskrit, describes the descent of a god into the human world? (6)

7 The least amount of fissile material that sustains a nuclear chain reaction is called the _____ mass (8)

13 What type of portable hut was used by the Jews as a temple for the Ark of the Covenant whilst moving through desert land? (10)

16 In golf, what type of score is achieved by a golfer who scores a bogie or worse? (5,3)

18 What scientific term is used to explain why a speaker "whines" when a microphone is put near to it? (8)

19 What was the popular form of design for interior decor in the 1920s and 30s featuring streamlined contours? (3,4)

21 What type of blade was usually used in agriculture, said to be fixed to the wheels of Boudicca's chariot? (6)

23 In law, if a person owes a payment, and that payment is legally enforceable, then he is a _____ (6)

26 What is the usual term applied to a subdivision of one of the world's major religious divisions? (4)

1

____ ____

2

_____ _____

3

TIONMOTIONMOTIONMOTIONMOTIO

_____ _____

4

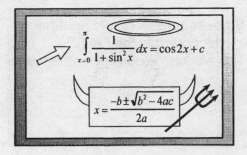

$$\int_{x=0}^{\pi} \frac{1}{1+\sin^2 x}\,dx = \cos 2x + c$$

$$x = \frac{-b \pm \sqrt{b^2 - 4ac}}{2a}$$

---- -----------

5

LOS ANGELES
SAN DIEGO
SAN JOSE
FRESNO

---------- -----

6

~~TUESDAY~~

THURSDAY ⬆

PETER
PAUL
NICHOLAS
CATHERINE
VITUS
STEPHEN
MICHAEL

------ --- ------

Blacken out those segments on the right-hand
page that are letter coded to the FALSE
statements. This will form a correct mathematical
sum.

True False

A   KLM is the national airline of Belgium   ☐ ☐

B   There are six states of Australia   ☐ ☐

C   Boxer Jack Dempsey's nickname was   ☐ ☐
     "the Manassa Mauler"

D   Sublimation is the process of turning   ☐ ☐
     from a gas to a solid (or vice versa)

E   The flag of Libya is coloured black   ☐ ☐
     and green

F   Tommy Dorsey, J. J. Johnson and   ☐ ☐
     Glen Miller all played the oboe

G   Wagner's *Aida* was first performed at   ☐ ☐
     the opening of the Suez Canal

H   Neptune is the planet eighth furthest   ☐ ☐
     from the Sun in the Solar System

J   There are twenty-seven cervical   ☐ ☐
     vertebrae in the human neck

K   Halifax is the capital of the Canadian   ☐ ☐
     province of Nova Scotia

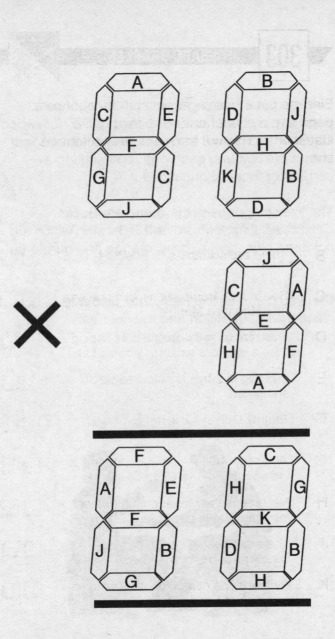

Five men at a board games club meet once a week to play their favourite board game *Hollywood Quest*. In this game, each space is colour coded one of five colours, each one representing a certain category of questions.

The five categories in the game are Books, Celebrities, Films, Music and Television which are coloured blue, green, grey, orange and purple (in some order).

Can you name all five men, their favourite categories of question and the colours represented by those categories?

CLUES

1. Mr Everett prefers the purple coloured squares.

2. Mr Harper likes the Films category best, which is not the blue neither the orange squares.

3. John Sanders doesn't like literature-based questions.

4. Patrick's favourite colour is the blue (this is not the colour of the TV questions).

5. The grey squares indicate the player must answer a question about Books, and you won't find Mr Erwin landing on these if he can help it.

6. Graham prefers the Celebrities category.

7. James avoids the green and orange squares.

STARTING HINTS

a. Clues 1, 2 and 5 should help you to work out the colour favoured by Mr Harper.

b. Work out John Sanders's favourite colour.

c. You should now be able to work out the colours for all five subjects. Now start matching these up to the names. (Kendal is the fifth surname.)

Forename	Surname	Colour	Category
Graham			
James			
John			
Patrick			
Paul			

Your task is to match up the show-stopping songs
below with the famous musicals that they appear
in.

1   *Get Me to the Church on Time*

2   *Luck Be a Lady*

3   *Wouldn't It Be Loverly*

4   *When I Marry Mr. Snow*

5   *Sit Down, You're Rocking the Boat*

6   *Anything You Can Do*

7   *Some Enchanted Evening*

8   *If They Could See Me Now*

9   *If I Loved You*

10 *You'll Never Walk Alone*

11 *A Bushel and a Peck*

12 *There is Nothing Like a Dame*

13 *I Could Have Danced All Night*

14 *There's No Business Like Show Business*

15 *Younger Than Springtime*

16 *Rhythm of Life*

17 *Doin' What Comes Naturally*

18 *I'm Gonna Wash That Man Right Outa My Hair*

19 *Money, Money*

20 *Hey Big Spender!*

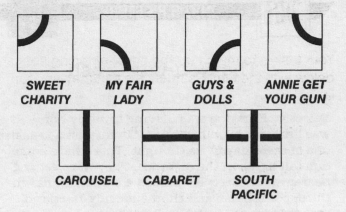

SWEET CHARITY **MY FAIR LADY** **GUYS & DOLLS** **ANNIE GET YOUR GUN**

CAROUSEL **CABARET** **SOUTH PACIFIC**

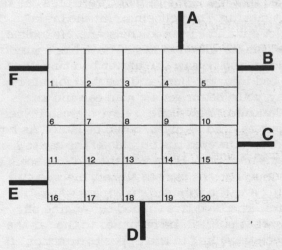

Your answer :
Pipe __ connects to pipe __
Pipe __ connects to pipe __
Pipe __ connects to pipe __

The Non-Car Crash

Detective Hartland was driving towards home. It was dark, foggy and raining. "I must get a transfer one of these days," he thought. There were some dim tail lights in the distance. They were getting nearer and nearer. He passed a stationary car in the opposite lane, and then suddenly Hartland realised that the lights in front were on a car that wasn't moving. The policeman hit the brakes.

He got out and surveyed the scene. He looked first at the car ahead of him. The driver's window was down and he saw the driver had sustained some bad injuries. Hartland reached for his radio. "Penny, you'd better get a squad car and an ambulance to Fields Lane. I have a crash driver with severe head injuries, could be fatal." As he waited, he surveyed the outside of the car to look for signs of impact. However, there didn't seem to be a scratch on the car but the engine was still running and the windscreen wipers were still working. The Detective turned the engine off.

Somewhat puzzled, he returned to the car that had been travelling in the opposite direction. It was some twenty yards down the road. The situation was much the same – the driver was badly hurt, wipers and engine still working, but no sign of any damage to the car.

At that point, a squad car turned up. "Hello sir," said the officer, "I was in the district so I thought

I'd assist. Looks nasty."

"Yes," said Hartland, "not a pretty sight. I thought this was a typical crash situation. Bad weather, narrow road, all the usual characteristics. But judging by the unharmed paintwork, I'll have to think again."

The officer had an idea. "I think I know what might have happened, sir. I've heard of a couple of similar accidents happening. I bet it was a shock to them, poor souls."

Can you suggest to the Detective what the most likely explanation for this situation might be?

Clues to ten of the longest words that we
managed to find :

1	*Copy, impersonate*
2	*Hurt and mutilated*
3	*Turned the lights down*
4	*Sudden*
5	*Arbitrated between sides*
6	*Reflect upon*
7	*Split into halves*
8	*Lead chloride mineral*
9	*Gave out sound*
10	*Believed to be, thought*

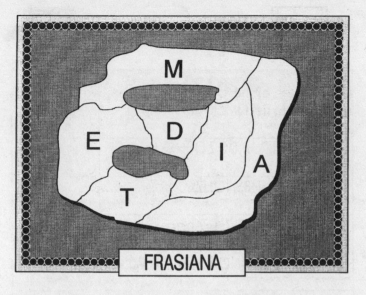

FRASIANA

Other words of five letters or more (find up to another 20) :

308   MISSING LINKS

WHO?	GUESSES
INTQMZKHRS	12
RDQHZKHRDC ZQSHBKDR	10
UHBSNQHZM	8
MHBJMZLD ANY	6
DCVHM CQNNC CHCM'S DMC	4
BNOODQEHDKC	2

WHAT?	GUESSES
LZHK NQCDQ	12
GNROHSZK ENNC	10
RHFMZSTQD	8
BNBJDQDK	6
AQDZJEZRS	4
JDKKNFF	2

386

WHERE?	GUESSES
ZKLZ LZSDQ NE DQZRLTR...	12
...ZMC RHQ SGNLZR LNQD	10
GNLD NE Z CHBSHNMZQX	8
SGHQSX-EHUD BNKKDFDR	6
QGNCDR RBGNKZQRGHOR	4
NKCDRS HM AQHSZHM	2

WHEN?	GUESSES
SZWHMF HRRTD	12
DZRS HMCHZ BNLOZMX	10
ZMSH AQHSHRG	8
ONQS	6
AQDV TO SQNTAKD	4
LZC ZR Z GZSSDQ	2

For each of the statements below, put your guesstimated answer in the appropriate box on the opposite page.

A   How many times stronger is the gravitational field of the Earth than that of the moon?

B   How many inches tall was the tallest ever American President, Abraham Lincoln?

C   How many Crusades were there?

D   How many thousands of elephants does Zaire have?

E   What is the maximum score in a frame of ten pin bowling?

F   How many different signs are there in the Chinese version of the zodiac?

G   How many dominoes are there in a full set?

H   How many stars are there in the consellation of Hydra, the largest in the sky?

J   How many planes did the (Red) Baron von Richthofen shoot down?

K   What is the average temperature (degrees F) in Norilsk, Russia?

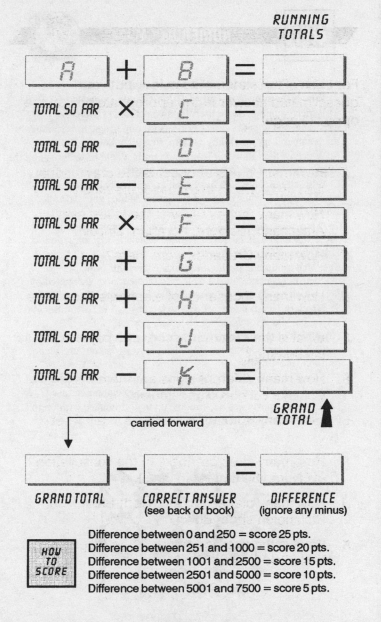

RUNNING
TOTALS

A	+	B	=	
TOTAL SO FAR	×	C	=	
TOTAL SO FAR	—	D	=	
TOTAL SO FAR	—	E	=	
TOTAL SO FAR	×	F	=	
TOTAL SO FAR	+	G	=	
TOTAL SO FAR	+	H	=	
TOTAL SO FAR	+	J	=	
TOTAL SO FAR	—	K	=	

GRAND
TOTAL

carried forward

	—		=	
GRAND TOTAL		CORRECT ANSWER		DIFFERENCE
		(see back of book)		(ignore any minus)

HOW TO SCORE

Difference between 0 and 250 = score 25 pts.
Difference between 251 and 1000 = score 20 pts.
Difference between 1001 and 2500 = score 15 pts.
Difference between 2501 and 5000 = score 10 pts.
Difference between 5001 and 7500 = score 5 pts.

1) Vampire is to wooden stake, as werewolf is to what?

2) Who is the subject of Billy Joel's hit single *Uptown Girl*?

3) Which country's name literally means Land of Silver?

4) Montego Bay is the subject of several pop songs, most famously the Number 3 hit for Bobby Bloom. In which country is it?

5) Which of the following Roman sections would have contained the most men – a cohort, a legion, or a century?

6) What chemical, which has etymological roots from the Greek word for green, gives the colour of many plants, grasses, and flowers?

7) A previous incarnation of which famous English landmark, the subject of a famous nursery rhyme, is now a tourist attraction in Lake Havasu City, Arizona?

8) Which modern household appliance uses this principle – a magnetron generates waves of a specific frequency (scattered by a fan) which excite any water molecules they come to?

9) Which (alleged) murderer did Jack Ruby kill in November 1963 saying he "did it for Jackie"?

10) Which of the six great wine-producing areas of France is further divided into many districts, of which the most famous are Medoc, St Emilion, and Graves?

11) In which field event is the women's world record greater than that of the men's because of the difference in equipment used?

12) In which sport does a game last up to 56 minutes, with up to 8 periods (or chukkas) lasting 7 minutes each?

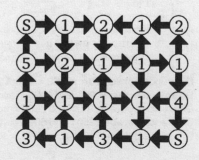

LAP 32

There are no time limits on this lap.

To score each puzzle, refer to the summary on pages 269–270. The maximum scores available are shown below.

	MAX.	SCORE
QUIZWORD	25	
REBUS CHALLENGE	30	
SAFE CRACKER	20	
LOGIC PROBLEM	20	
IN THE PIPELINE	20	
CRIME STORY	25	
WORD ISLAND	30	
MISSING LINKS	30	
NUMEROLOGY	25	
MAGNIFICENT MAZE	25	
TOTAL (max. 250)		

TARGET TO BEAT – 170 points

ACROSS

1 Which river of Guyana is also the proper name of "brown" sugar? (8)

5 What is a bicycle designed to be ridden by two people called? (6)

10 Which key is usually at the top-right of the main block of keys on a standard computer keyboard? (9)

11 What type of chord is formed by playing three notes with gaps of three and four semitones between them? (5)

12 Which British writer, real name Eric Blair, wrote *Animal Farm* and *Nineteen Eighty-four*? (6)

13 In Greek mythology, who took 20 years to return home from the Trojan War, as recounted in a famous Homer epic? (8)

15 With what is a violin bow usually strung? (9)

17 In the card game pinochle, what is the lowest card value used? (4)

20 What symbol, at the beginning of a musical stave, indicates the particular range of notes used? (4)

21 What type of land, such as the Fens and the Everglades, has its water table near the surface of the ground? (9)

24 Which Indian prince, ranking above rajah, usually was in charge of his own state? (8)

25 Which period of the Christian Calendar of some four weeks prepares for Christmas? (6)

28 Which part of the body was used to indicate to a gladiator whether he should kill his defeated opponent? (5)

29 What model of motor-car, similar to a coupe, usually has two doors and a folding top? (9)

30 Which US vocalist had hits with *It Hurts So Much*, *Distant Drums* and *I Love You Because* in the 1960s? (6)

31 What Indian dish of rice, onions and spices has a European version made using rice, fish and boiled eggs? (8)

DOWN

1 One who owes money (6)

2 Which bird of the American tropics is the largest member of the parrot family? (5)

3 What word could possibly mean "fidgety" and "without stopping"? (8)

4 In the paper industry what name is usually given to a bundle of 480 sheets of paper? (4)

6 This word means "very nearly" (6)

7 Which flower takes its name from the French for "lion's tooth"? (9)

8 Wild Bill Hickok and Wyatt Earp were famous Western ____, famed for their shooting skills (8)

9 How a diver jumps into things? (4,5)

14 A travelling salesman who claims to have some amazing, too-good-to-be-true bargains (5-4)

16 A period of time, usually several hours, during which guests are particularly welcome to take hospitality (4-5)

18 What type of short sword, curved in shape and widest nearest the point, was used by the Turks? (8)

19 Which metallurgical process bonds layers of different metals together, to produce things such as rolled gold? (8)

22 If woofers provide the bass, what do tweeters provide? (6)

23 12 Across based his *Pygmalion* on the mythological character of the same name who fell in love with Galatea, a ____ (6)

26 Which Swiss mathematician was famous for solving the topological Konigsberg Bridge problem? (5)

27 Which wooden double-reed instrument has a range of over two octaves (up to a tone below middle C) using over fifteen keys? (4)

393

1 INFIN ITIVE

_ _ _ _ _   _ _ _ _ _ _ _ _

S H	OO
TI	NG

2

_ _ _ _ _ _ _ _   _ _ _ _ _ _

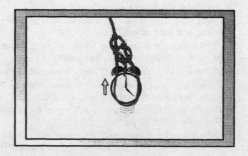

3

_ _ _ _ _   _ _ _   _ _ _ _ _

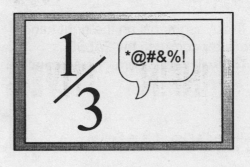

_ _ _ _ _ _ _ _ _ _ _ _ _ _ _

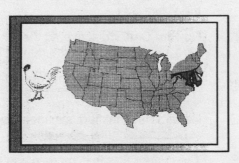

_ _ _ _ _ _ _ _ _ _ _ _ _ _ _

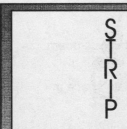

_ _ _ _ _ _ _ _ _ _ _ _ _ _ _

Blacken out those segments on the right-hand page that are letter coded to the FALSE statements. This will form a correct mathematical sum.

True False

A J. F. Kennedy Airport is in Dallas, Texas ☐ ☐

B The Boston baseball team is called the White Sox ☐ ☐

C Howard Carter discovered the sarcophagus of Tutankhamun in 1924 ☐ ☐

D The year 2000 will be the Year of the Dragon in the Chinese calendar ☐ ☐

E Nepal's national flag is made of two separate triangular pennants ☐ ☐

F The liqueur Pastis is made using the blackcurrant plant ☐ ☐

G Beethoven's second opera was *Fidelio* ☐ ☐

H W. H. Auden wrote the famous poem *Tell Me the Truth About Love* ☐ ☐

J The dog Laika was put into space in *Sputnik 11* in November 1957 ☐ ☐

K A polygon can speak many languages ☐ ☐

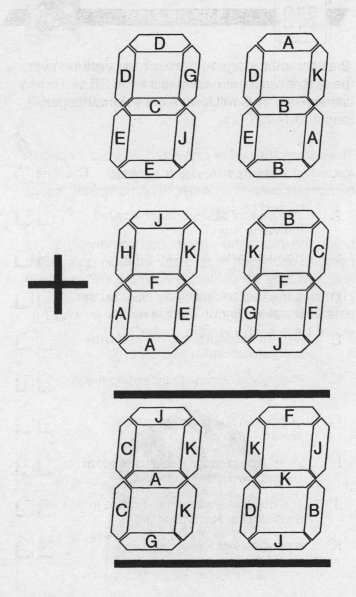

LOGIC PROBLEM

The infamous Judge Anderson has presided over the sentencing of five criminals today. Their names are Bruiser Bill, Cad Clive, Freaky Fred, Slippery Sam and Tough Tim.

The crimes they were convicted of are deception, forgery, poaching, rustling and treason. The five sentences meted out were, in no particular order, 3, 6, 7, 10 and 15 years.

Using the information given, can you match a name to each picture and say what his crime was and how long his sentence was? If a criminal says "Tim was the rustler" you may assume that the person speaking is not Tim the rustler (or else he would have said "I am the rustler").

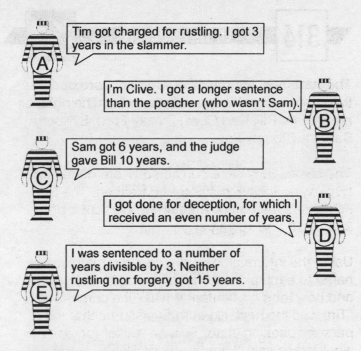

STARTING HINTS

a. Use the information given by B, D and E to find which crime carried the longest sentence.

b. Use A, C and E's clues to work out Bill's sentence. Which picture is he?

Diagram	Name	Crime	Sentence
Picture A			
Picture B			
Picture C			
Picture D			
Picutre E			

IN THE PIPELINE

Your task is to connect the famous sportspeople with their individual specialist sport on the right.

1   Merlene Ottey
2   Michael Stich
3   Jose Maria Olazabal
4   Mario Andretti
5   Ingrid Kristiansen
6   Sally Gunnell
7   Viktor Petrenko
8   Chris Boardman
9   Riccardo Patrese
10 Katarina Witt
11 Ben Crenshaw
12 Emerson Fittipaldi
13 Carl Lewis
14 Mats Wilander
15 Matt Biondi
16 Mark Spitz
17 Greg LeMond
18 Ben Johnson
19 Leroy Burrell
20 Hannah Mandlikova

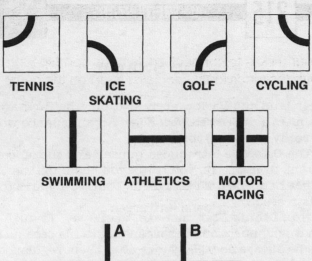

TENNIS   ICE   GOLF   CYCLING
          SKATING

SWIMMING   ATHLETICS   MOTOR
                         RACING

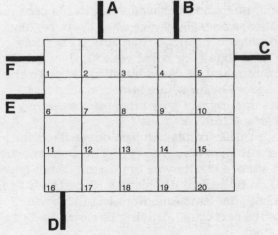

Your answer :

Pipe __ connects to pipe __

Pipe __ connects to pipe __

Pipe __ connects to pipe __

The Swarm

Hartland and Barlow arrived at 63, The Parkway, to meet a distressed Mrs Edge. An ambulance was already attending the scene.

The Detective introduced himself and the officer to the woman. "Do you think you could tell me what happened, Mrs Edge? Of course, if you're too distressed..."

"No, I think I can manage, thank you. Frank, that's my husband, was attending to his bees just as he always does. He looks after them regularly and he was out in the garden collecting some honey. Well today, for some reason, they decided to turn on him and he came bursting through the back door with the whole swarm in chase. I couldn't understand why after ten years they would attack him like that."

"Well, I think things can just occur like that. Nature will have it's own way." The Detective tried to find a more kindly way of putting it, but there was no point avoiding the truth. Sometimes these things happen. Hartland went to talk to the ambulance personnel, leaving Barlow to talk to the woman.

"It's such unfortunate timing as well," the woman added.

"What do mean, Mrs Edge?" asked Barlow.

"Well it was his 50th birthday just yesterday. He was looking so cheerful, opening his presents and having the family around him. Daniel and Mary, our children, had just come back from six months in Malaga. He was so pleased to see them and they bought some lovely duty-free presents for Frank. We had a lovely tea and then later that day..."

"Erm, I'm sorry to interrupt you, Mrs Edge, but... Oh, here comes the Detective now."

Hartland returned to say his goodbyes. "The ambulance staff say your husband should be fine, Mrs Edge. But I must say this – spending five minutes in that ambulance has given me an idea that the action of his bees is more understandable than it first seemed!"

Can you deduce what Frank Edge did wrong to make the bees attack him?

Clues to ten of the longest words that we managed to find :

1	'White elephant' objects are...
2	One holding a sublease
3	Without heartbeat?
4	Soapy spheres
5	Small, smooth pieces of rock
6	Fencing swords
7	Is dormant
8	Wishes one well
9	A pretty (French?) woman
10	The bo tree

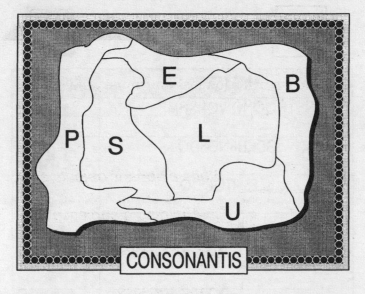

CONSONANTIS

Other words of five letters or more (find up to
another 20) :

WHO?	GUESSES
LHQQNQ VQHSHMF	12
GDKHBNOSDQ	10
KZRS RTOODQ	8
ZQBGHSDBS	6
HSZKHZM	4
LNMZ KHRZ	2

WHAT?	GUESSES
LZFMDSHB	12
RHWSDDM CHFHSR	10
OHM	8
GNKNFQZL	6
DWOHQX CZSD	4
CHMDQ'R BKTA EHQRS	2

WHERE?	GUESSES
BNQCHKKDQZ	12
ZBNMBZFTZ	10
KZJD SHSHBZBZ	8
UNKBZMHB	6
BZOD GNQM	4
RNTSG ZLDQHBZ	2

WHEN?	GUESSES
QDRSZQS DHFGSDDM-MHMDSX-RHW	12
MNS 'RHWSDDM, 'ENQSX, 'ENQSX-ENTQ	10
ZTRSQZKHZ ZS RSZQS NE BDMSTQX	8
RSZQSR VHSG Z SNQBG	6
VHMSDQ UDQRHNM SNN	4
EHUD QHMFR	2

For each of the statements below, put your guesstimated answer in the appropriate box on the opposite page.

A How many Labours did Hercules (or Heracles) have to perform?

B How many chambers are there in the heart?

C Which number appeared in the title of Joseph Heller's most famous book?

D How many feet are there in a nautical fathom?

E The fuel coke is made up of how many per cent carbon?

F How many inches high is the golden Oscar statue?

G How old was Ronald Reagan at his first inauguration as President?

H What percentage of Canadians speak French?

J How many million tourists visited Eurodisney, Paris in 1992?

K How many inches long is the average femur, also called the thigh bone?

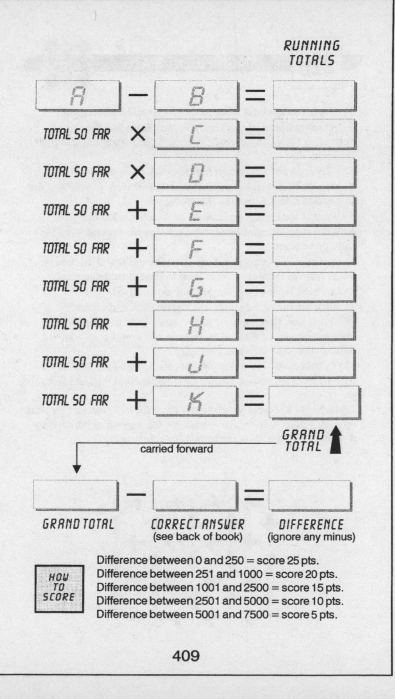

RUNNING TOTALS

A $-$ B $=$

TOTAL SO FAR $\times$ C $=$

TOTAL SO FAR $\times$ D $=$

TOTAL SO FAR $+$ E $=$

TOTAL SO FAR $+$ F $=$

TOTAL SO FAR $+$ G $=$

TOTAL SO FAR $-$ H $=$

TOTAL SO FAR $+$ J $=$

TOTAL SO FAR $+$ K $=$

GRAND TOTAL

carried forward

$-$ $=$

GRAND TOTAL   CORRECT ANSWER   DIFFERENCE
                  (see back of book)   (ignore any minus)

HOW TO SCORE

Difference between 0 and 250 = score 25 pts.
Difference between 251 and 1000 = score 20 pts.
Difference between 1001 and 2500 = score 15 pts.
Difference between 2501 and 5000 = score 10 pts.
Difference between 5001 and 7500 = score 5 pts.

409

1) In what subject did *Alice* author Lewis Carroll lecture?

2) Which member of the *Monty Python* team had the job of delivering their catchphrase "And now for something completely different..."?

3) Why is Nepal's flag different to every other nation's?

4) Manchester, Dorchester, and Winchester were so suffixed due to which evident feature in these cities?

5) What is the British equivalent of America's Delta Force?

6) What type of connoisseur would know his muscat from his sauvignon blanc?

7) For recycling purposes, how does one tell that a drinks can is made from aluminium, rather than from less valuable steel?

8) In which layer of the atmosphere do we live?

9) What are the Avesta, Granth, Katabi Ikan and Koran?

10) What was first made by a physician from tree bark in the Venezuelan city of Ciudad Bolivar in 1824, and is an additive now used in cocktails and pink gin?

11) In basketball, how many points are scored for a basket thrown from a distance greater than 23 feet and 9 inches from the target?

12) Which 1851 trophy, originally the *Hundred Guinea Cup*, has only ever been won by two countries, the second of which only won in 1983 with John Bertram's boat *Australia II*?

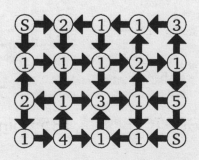

LAP 33

There are no time limits on this lap.

To score each puzzle, refer to the summary on pages 269–270. The maximum scores available are shown below.

	MAX.	SCORE
QUIZWORD	25	
REBUS CHALLENGE	30	
SAFE CRACKER	20	
LOGIC PROBLEM	20	
IN THE PIPELINE	20	
CRIME STORY	25	
WORD ISLAND	30	
MISSING LINKS	30	
NUMEROLOGY	25	
MAGNIFICENT MAZE	25	
TOTAL (max. 250)		

TARGET TO BEAT – 185 points

1		2		3		4		■	5	6		7		8

ACROSS

1 Which religious post for a cleric takes its name from *cappella*, the Latin for "short cloak"? (8)

5 What document is issued in some countries to all adults to provide proof of identity for a variety of purposes? (1,1,4)

10 Of what do humans have 20 before their adult 32 come through? (4,5)

11 What is the last letter of the Greek alphabet? (5)

12 What, in physics, is defined as "the capacity of matter to perform work"? (6)

13 In history, rib bones of animals were tied to the feet. Nowadays, we use a steel blade as an _____ _____ (3,5)

15 In what form is low-density polyethylene (or LDPE) normally sold in your local supermarket? (9)

17 In mathematics, a Mobius band is a topological shape with one side and one _____ (4)

412

20 What mathematical solid has twelve edges of equal length and six congruent faces? (4)

21 Which symbol, a five-pointed star, is one of the most significant used in witchcraft? (9)

24 What word, now the name of a car, was originally used to describe a warship smaller than a frigate with one tier of guns? (8)

25 What lizard, primarily of the Americas, lends its name to a dinosaur whose distinctive jaws have similar teeth? (6)

28 What is the French word for "school"? (5)

29 In fluid mechanics, what property measures how resistant a fluid is to flowing? (9)

30 What is the capital of Oman? (6)

31 What event occurs when the year is divisible by 4 or 400 but not by 100? (4,4)

DOWN

1 What did Athena, the Greek mythological goddess, change the rope that Arachne had attempted to hang herself with into? (6)

2 To walk at a leisurely pace (5)

3 What legal term describes one who carries out a law suit? (8)

4 What is the common name given to several species of wild Asian goat of the genus *Capra*? (4)

6 What is the general term for the medical condition of having excess fluid in the body tissue or organs? (6)

7 What is Queen Elizabeth II of England's second name? (9)

8 In mathematics, what is the maximum length for a chord of a given circle called? (8)

9 Which popular commodity was brought to Europe by Cortez, who had learnt of it from the Aztecs? (9)

14 Which word means "in operation" or "producing the effect required"? (9)

16 Requiring a lot of effort (9)

18 What frozen food is made from cream, milk, sugar and flavourings? (3,5)

19 The Australian aborigines forbid anyone to marry someone from a different _____ _____ (3,5)

22 What is the unit of currency of Spain? (6)

23 For which occupation did F. W. De Klerk, Juan Melendez, Nelson Mandela and Hillary Clinton train? (6)

26 In the books by A. A. Milne, what was the name of Christopher Robin's female companion? (5)

27 What geographical word connects Man, Royale, Wight, Presque, Belle, Ely and Pines? (4)

1

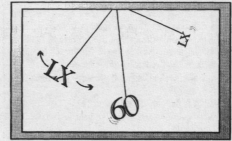

_ _ _ _ _ _ _ _   _ _ _ _ _ _ _

RUBBISH

WANT

2

_ _ _ _ _ _   _ _ _   _ _ _ _   _ _ _

3

1 ANOTHER
1 ANOTHER
1 ANOTHER
1 ANOTHER
1 ANOTHER
1 ANOTHER

_ _ _   _ _   _ _ _   _ _ _   _ _ _ _   _

_ _ _ _ _   _ _   _ _ _ _ _ _ _

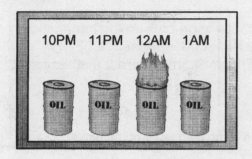

10PM 11PM 12AM 1AM

OIL OIL OIL OIL

4

---- --- -------- ---

5

VATNIMBI

------- - -------

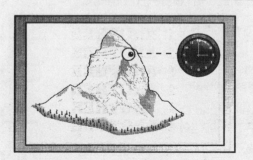

6

---- ------- ----

Blacken out those segments on the right-hand page that are letter coded to the FALSE statements. This will form a correct mathematical sum.

True False

A   Epsilon is the third letter of the Greek alphabet   ☐ ☐

B   At the Battle of Rourke's Drift in 1879, 4000 British repelled 140 Zulus   ☐ ☐

C   Romanian dictator Ceaucescu was assassinated on Christmas Day, 1982   ☐ ☐

D   A marguerita is made from tequila, cointreau and lemon juice   ☐ ☐

E   The term 'Glasnost' means 'truth' in Russian   ☐ ☐

F   Alliteration is the formation of a word that imitates the sound it represents   ☐ ☐

G   Al Pacino won a '93 Academy Award for his role in *Scent of a Woman*   ☐ ☐

H   No British Prime Minister has ever been assassinated   ☐ ☐

J   The Walker and Curtis Cups are famous golfing trophies   ☐ ☐

K   In music, *largo* means 'increase the tempo'   ☐ ☐

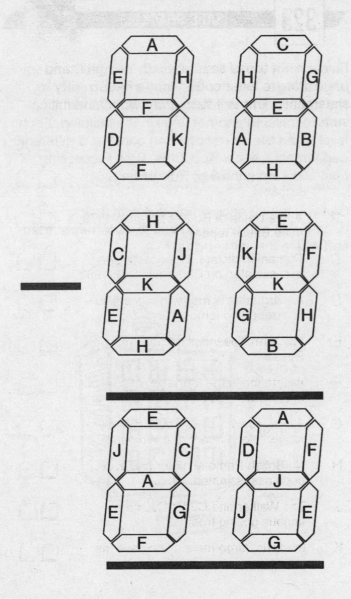

Five employees of the Labyrinth Widget Company are waiting to use the lift. **They are currently in the department in which they work**, and they wish to travel to another level in the building. Each level of the five storey building contains a different department – either Accounts, Data Processing, Marketing, Personnel or Purchasing.

Can you match each employee with their department and tell us on which level they started and where they will end up?

Level 5
Level 4
Level 3
Level 2
Level 1

CLUES

1. Jonathan (who works in Data Processing) went up three levels.

2. The Purchasing department is situated on Level 2 of the building.

3. The journey that started on Level 3 was destined to go downwards.

4. Annabel (who is not from Marketing) went up one level during her journey.

5. The man from Accounts went down two levels.

6. One journey went from Level 2 to Level 1.

7. Neither Melanie nor Norman works on Level 3.

STARTING HINTS

a. Use clues 1 and 2 immediately to deduce Jonathan's level.

b. Now have a good look at the other clues, number 6 especially – can you deduce the start and end positions of all the journeys?

Worker	Dept.	From floor	To floor
Annabel			
Jonathan			
Melanie			
Norman			
Steve			

Your task is to match the famous painters on the right with their equally famous paintings, below.

1   *The Crucifixion*

2   *Mona Lisa*

3   *Bathers*

4   *The Persistence of Memory*

5   *The Sunflowers*

6   *Ceiling of the Sistine Chapel*

7   *The Last Supper*

8   *Madonna of the Kings*

9   *Leda and the Swan*

10 *Starry Night*

11 *Le Jardinier*

12 *The Last Judgement*

13 *Wyoming*

14 *Water Lilies*

15 *Christ of St. John on the Cross*

16 *The Conversion of St. Paul*

17 *Self Portrait with Bandaged Ear*

18 *Night Cafe*

19 *Autumn Rhythm*

20 *Impression: Sunrise*

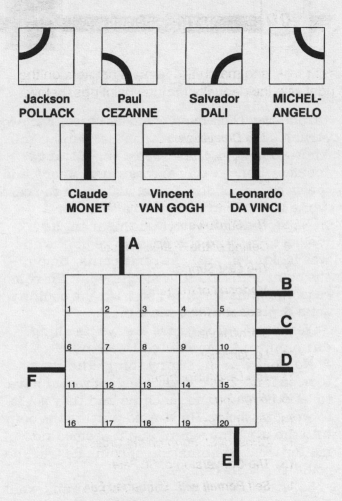

Jackson
POLLACK

Paul
CEZANNE

Salvador
DALI

MICHEL-
ANGELO

Claude
MONET

Vincent
VAN GOGH

Leonardo
DA VINCI

A

B

C

D

F

E

1 2 3 4 5
6 7 8 9 10
11 12 13 14 15
16 17 18 19 20

Your answer :
Pipe __ connects to pipe __
Pipe __ connects to pipe __
Pipe __ connects to pipe __

421

The Mysterious Coins

On the way back from their last case, Barlow struck up conversation with Hartland. "You know, Detective, there was a very strange incident I once came across when Wendy and me were on holiday. I was waiting in the car while Wendy had gone into a store for a newspaper when I noticed this man, he looked to be from the Arabian region, who was looking intently at some coins. He put the coins into this cola machine but for some reason, no matter what he tried, he couldn't get a drink out of the machine."

"Yeah, those things are always breaking down on me," commented Hartland.

"No, that was the funny thing. The chap took so long that occasionally he would have to let others use the machine and they got it to work perfectly. He started putting the coins into the machine again, and it seemed no matter what combination of coins he tried he couldn't get his can.

"So, eventually I got out of the car and went over to help him. The man held out his hand, so I took the right change from his palm and put the coins in the machine. I heard a click, I motioned to the man to make his selection, the man pressed the relevant button and out popped a can.

"Then the man said 'Thank you very much, effendi. I do not have trouble like this in other countries I go to.' We got chatting for a while. Apparently he was quite well travelled. He'd been to many different Western countries over a period of around twenty years. Yet he wasn't used to having such difficulty with such a simple task. A nice chap."

"Now I think I know where you went for your holidays," smiled Hartland.

Can you work out where Barlow was on holiday?

Clues to ten of the longest words that we managed to find :

1	Those who mark skin
2	Italian ice-cream
3	Mathematical subject
4	Type of electricity
5	Short, jumpy musical notes
6	Chocolate powder
7	Disease of the ear
8	Clue '6' comes from this
9	Helps out
10	Blackcurrant flavouring

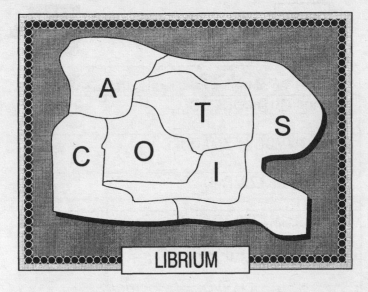

A C O T I S

LIBRIUM

Other words of five letters or more (find up to another 20) :

MISSING LINKS

WHO?	GUESSES
ZMSH–ONRSLDM	12
NVMDC AX ZQATBJKD	10
KZRZFMD	8
LNMCZXR ZQD AZC	6
NUDQVDHFGS ZMC OQNTC NE HS	4
BZQSNNM BZS	2

WHAT?	GUESSES
MHMDSX-EHUD ODQBDMS BZQANM CHNWHCD	12
RHW-DHFGS-RDUDM CZXR	10
OGNANR ZMC CDHLNR	8
ENTQ NE MHMD	6
BQZSDQR	4
QDC	2

WHERE?	GUESSES
GTCRNM & DZRS	12
RSZSDM HRKZMC	10
NMBD BZOHSZK	8
RSZSD SNN	6
DLOHQD RSZSD ATHKCHMF	4
AHF ZOOKD	2

WHEN?	GUESSES
AQZYHK W SGQDD	12
QHLDS	10
KZRS VZR HM TRZ	8
EHEZ	6
ENTQ XDZQR	4
ENNSAZKK	2

For each of the statements below, put your guesstimated answer in the appropriate box on the opposite page.

R On how many hills is Rome said to stand?

B What isotope of carbon is used in the technique of carbon dating?

C How many people comprise a court jury in major legal cases?

D How many minutes did the fastest swim across the English Channel take?

E How many heads did Cerberus (the dog that guarded the entrance to Hades) have?

F How many feet long was a diplodocus?

G 31 degrees Celsius is how many degrees in Fahrenheit?

H How many bones are there in the human body?

J How many letters are there in the official, poetic name for Bangkok City?

K How many people in the UK are US dollar billionaires?

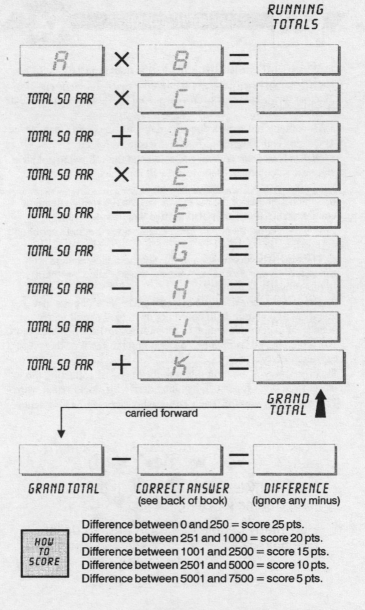

RUNNING TOTALS

A × B =

TOTAL SO FAR × C =

TOTAL SO FAR + D =

TOTAL SO FAR × E =

TOTAL SO FAR − F =

TOTAL SO FAR − G =

TOTAL SO FAR − H =

TOTAL SO FAR − J =

TOTAL SO FAR + K =

GRAND TOTAL

carried forward

GRAND TOTAL − CORRECT ANSWER (see back of book) = DIFFERENCE (ignore any minus)

HOW TO SCORE

Difference between 0 and 250 = score 25 pts.
Difference between 251 and 1000 = score 20 pts.
Difference between 1001 and 2500 = score 15 pts.
Difference between 2501 and 5000 = score 10 pts.
Difference between 5001 and 7500 = score 5 pts.

1) Which J.M. Barrie book provides the quotation "All children except one grow up" in its opening line?

2) What theatrical profession was shared by Hamlet's Yorick and Henry I's Rahere?

3) How many red stripes does the flag known as *Old Glory* have?

4) Queens is the largest of five districts in which city?

5) Which European country once counted the following countries amongst its colonies – Jamaica, the Philippines, Trinidad, and virtually every South American country?

6) Which member of the cat family has the alternative name of cougar, and is sometimes also termed the mountain lion?

7) In which constituent part of an engine does the fuel vapour and air mix?

8) The magnetic storms seen in the Southern Hemisphere are called the *Aurora Australis*. What are the so-called Northern Lights properly known as?

9) The *Index Librorum Prohibitorum* was a list of books that members of a certain faith could not own, read or sell under penalty of excommunication (a threat lifted in 1966). Which faith?

10) Which pepper is obtained by grinding the seeds of the capsicum berry?

11) Fromology is the term given to the hobby of collecting the labels from what foodstuff, its name derived from a French word?

12) How many umpires are used in today's cricket Test Matches?

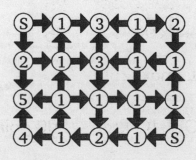

There are no time limits on this lap.

To score each puzzle, refer to the summary on pages 269–270. The maximum scores available are shown below.

	MAX.	SCORE
QUIZWORD	25	
REBUS CHALLENGE	30	
SAFE CRACKER	20	
LOGIC PROBLEM	20	
IN THE PIPELINE	20	
CRIME STORY	25	
WORD ISLAND	30	
MISSING LINKS	30	
NUMEROLOGY	25	
MAGNIFICENT MAZE	25	
TOTAL (max. 250)		

TARGET TO BEAT – 200 points

1	2	3	4	5	6	7	8

(Crossword grid with numbered cells: 1, 2, 3, 4, 5, 6, 7, 8, 9, 10, 11, 12, 13, 14, 15, 16, 17, 18, 19, 20, 21, 22, 23, 24, 25, 26, 27, 28, 29, 30)

ACROSS

9   In the brewing process, in which building are the hops or malt dried? (4-5)

10   What is the Spanish word for "friend"? (5)

11   The largest one to create a disaster so far is Chernobyl (7)

12   In gambling, what type of bet pays out upon the selected racer finishing in the top two places? (4,3)

13   What drink is made from hot beer or spirits mixed with whole egg? (6)

14   Which alcohol is a colourless, viscous liquid, obtained as a by-product of soap making, and is used in the making of plastics? (8)

16   A ritual or ceremony performed to show that a person has reached one of the key stages of life (4)

17   _____ City, in southern Kansas, was famous for having Wyatt Earp as a chief deputy marshal (5)

18   In which direction are you going if your bearing is 090? (4)

22 Which American state is south of South Dakota, west of Iowa, north of Kansas, and east of Wyoming? (8)

24 The _____ family of birds has subfamilies which include lovebirds, macaws, lories and parakeets? (6)

27 In the United States, the land upon which a foreign _____ stands actually belongs to that country (7)

28 Which city, in the Seine-Maritime Department and on the English Channel, is a main French seaport? (2,5)

29 Which English phrase for a German submarine comes from the word *Unterseeboot*? (1-4)

30 Artificial, as in the title of Philip Massinger's 1639 play *The _____ Combat* (9)

DOWN

1 What is the name of the Stock Exchange of France? (6)

2 What is the French word for "snail"? (8)

3 Which word, now used in a wider context, originally defined city regions within which all Jews must reside? (7)

4 Which golden brown powder is made from about 20 spices including ginger, fenugreek, turmeric and cumin? (5)

5 What is the study of one's ancestors, as depicted in family trees, called? (9)

6 One of Irish dramatist Sean O'Casey's most famous plays is *Juno and the _____* (7)

7 One who watches a television programme (6)

8 What word is used to describe a person who can speak many languages? (8)

15 What is another name for what is normally termed the peanut (or ground nut)? (6-3)

16 The person who came second (6-2)

19 What is the (somewhat unusual) name for the F-111 jet fighter, capable of Mach 2? (8)

20 Used for hunting and tracking small animals, which hounds are known for their superb sense of smell? (7)

21 What type of knife, with a sharp heavy blade, is often used in the jungle? (7)

23 Which type of large monkey lives in open land in Africa and Arabia? (6)

25 Which range of the musical scale does the soprano use? (6)

26 A long, thick piece of timber (5)

433

1

___   ___

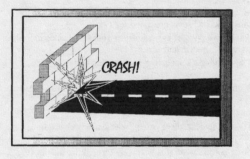

2

____   _____   _____

3

1	‖ IT
2	‖IG IT
3	NIG IT
4	NIGHT

____   _   _____   __   __

– – – – – – – – – – – –
– – – – – –

– – – – – – – – – – – –

– – – – – – – – – – – –
– – – – – – – – – –

435

Blacken out those segments on the right-hand page that are letter coded to the FALSE statements. This will form a correct mathematical sum.

True False

A   Franklin D. Roosevelt died of natural causes whilst in office as President   ☐ ☐

B   According to the Beaufort Scale, winds over 53 kph are hurricanes   ☐ ☐

C   Davy Crockett was killed at the Battle of the Alamo   ☐ ☐

D   The collective noun for owls is a 'murder'   ☐ ☐

E   The Latin name for the banana is *Ananas comosus*   ☐ ☐

F   Hyundai cars are made in Korea   ☐ ☐

G   Gauguin painted *Bathers* and *Le Jardinier*   ☐ ☐

H   The Radio Call Sign for the letter Y is Yellow   ☐ ☐

J   Symphony No. 8 in B Minor by Schubert is the Unfinished Symphony   ☐ ☐

K   Pyrographs on electric trains pick up current from an overhead power line   ☐ ☐

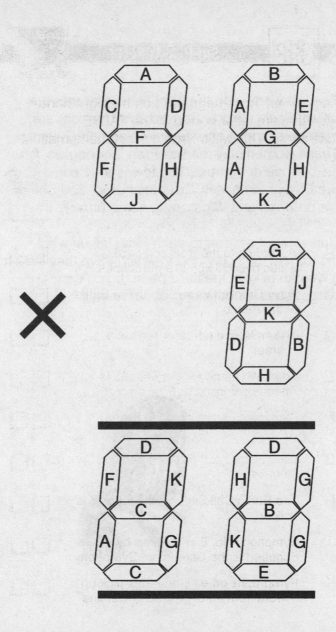

437

The five women on the right (whose names are Olivia, Paula, Rhona, Sandra and Theresa) are members of the Leicestershire Youth Orchestra. These women play the bassoon, cor anglais, flute, saxophone or trumpet. The towns they come from are Broughton Astley, Countesthorpe, Earl Shilton, Narborough and Wigston (in some order).

Can you put a name to each face, tell us what instrument they play and in which town they live? If a woman talks in the third person, you can assume she is not talking about herself.

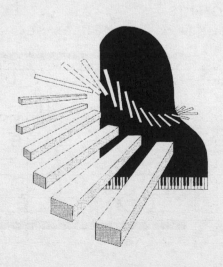

A

Olivia, who is not the cor anglais player, lives in Wigston.

I live in Narborough. I'm not the cor anglais player.

I don't live in Wigston. I play the trumpet. I'm not the Theresa who lives in Earl Shilton.

C

B

The saxophonist (who is not Theresa) lives in Broughton Astley.

D

Paula plays the flute. I'm Sandra, but I don't play cor anglais.

E

STARTING HINTS

a. You'll need the clues from A, B, C and E to tell you which picture is the Wigston woman.

b. Now see if you can find which pictures are the saxophonist and the cor anglais player.

Picture	Name	Home Town	Instrument
Picture A			
Picture B			
Picture C			
Picture D			
Picture E			

Your task is to connect the anatomical terms below with the area of the body in which they can be found.

1 Pituitary Gland

2 Malleus

3 Retina

4 Femur

5 Cerebrum

6 Fibula

7 Humerus

8 Tibia

9 Radius

10 Metatarsal

11 Dentine

12 Ulna

13 Phalange

14 Bicuspid

15 Hypothalamus

16 Aqueous Humour

17 Talus

18 Conjunctiva

19 Melanin

20 Cuboid

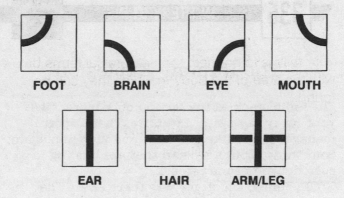

FOOT **BRAIN** **EYE** **MOUTH**

EAR **HAIR** **ARM/LEG**

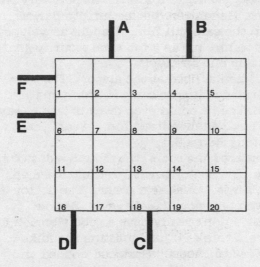

Your answer :

Pipe __ connects to pipe __

Pipe __ connects to pipe __

Pipe __ connects to pipe __

The Dummy Explosion

The radio crackled into action once more. "It's your lucky day again, Detective. That airport manager would like you to go and visit him again. Something about a woman they are holding in custody who's gone berserk."

"OK, Penny, I'm on my way there now." The Detective was getting to know the airport very well by this time. He muttered something to Barlow, who was in the car with him. "I might as well get the swines to hire me as a full time security guard. I'm practically one already!"

The policemen arrived at the airport. The now familiar airport manager came running up to them but before he could even draw breath to say anything Hartland dismissed him. "Yeah, yeah, we know. Custody Room 3."

As they entered the room, they found a doctor in attendance. The doctor turned to the policemen. "I'm sorry, gents, but she's a goner." The doctor let go of the woman's now lifeless wrist. Barlow winced. "Sir, I don't really have a good stomach for dead people. I think I'll just question the folks outside if that's all right." Hartland nodded and Barlow stepped out of the room.

Hartland began questioning the doctor. "What happened here then, Doctor...?"

"My name's Andrew Hall. Pleased to meet you," said the doctor. "Yes, apparently she came off the flight from Cuba, through customs and as she was about to leave the airport the plastic bag she was

carrying exploded. Of course, this caused her
death almost immediately."

"Well, it's quite common nowadays, isn't it? We'll
have to see if we can persuade the airport
manager to step up security. I'll be back in a
moment. I just want to see what my colleague is
doing."

"Rightio," said Hall.

Barlow had just finished talking to the airport
manager. "Well, seems like a standard terrorist
bombing case to me," said Hartland.

Barlow put on one of his quizzical looks. "What
do you mean, sir? It's nothing of the sort. I think
you've got the wrong end of the stick..."

**Can you work out what the misunderstanding is and
thus explain what happened to cause the woman's
death?**

443

Clues to ten of the longest words that we
managed to find :

1	*Mineral deposit on the teeth*
2	*Perform repeated calculations*
3	*To say again*
4	*Average over two matches*
5	*One who rues*
6	*That which is left behind*
7	*African amulet*
8	*To perform titration*
9	*Run away*
10	*Boat-racing meeting*

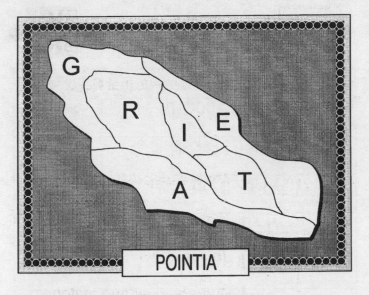

POINTIA

Other words of five letters or more (find up to another 20) :

445

WHO?	GUESSES
Z FDQLZM ADDQLTF	12
RVHRR (ZS EHQRS)	10
ZLDQHBZM (KZSDQ NM)	8
MNADK OQHYD	6
EZLNTR ENQLTKZ	4
QDKZSHUHSX	2

WHAT?	GUESSES
ZTFTRSD AZQSGNKCH	12
ZMMHUDQRZQX OQDRDMS	10
SVN HM DWHRSDMBD	8
GZQANTQ	6
SNQBG	4
EQDDCNL RXLANK	2

WHERE?	GUESSES
CDOZQSLDMSR	12
LZRRHE BDMSQZK	10
NVMR FTZCDKNTOD & LZQSHMHPTD	8
QGNMD UZKKDX VHMD	6
BGZSDZTW NM SGD KNHQD	4
BGZMMDK STMMDK KHMJ	2

WHEN?	GUESSES
DCVZQC RLHSG	12
BZQOZSGHZ	10
LZHCDM	8
ZOQHK EHESDDM MHMDSDDM-SVDKUD	6
AZMC OKZXDC NM	4
HBDADQF	2

For each of the statements below, put your guesstimated answer in the appropriate box on the opposite page.

A   How many movements does a symphony normally have?

B   How many legs does a crab have?

C   What percentage of the TVs in the USA are connected to a video?

D   How many Major titles has Jack Nicklaus won in his career?

E   How many metres wide is the mirror on the world's largest reflecting telescope?

F   How many TV stations were operating in the USA in 1948?

G   How many bottles of wine does France consume per head per annum?

H   How many years did Queen Victoria reign over Britain?

J   How many feet high is the General Sherman giant sequoia tree, the highest in the world?

K   How many million dollars did the 1987 film *Ishtar* lose?

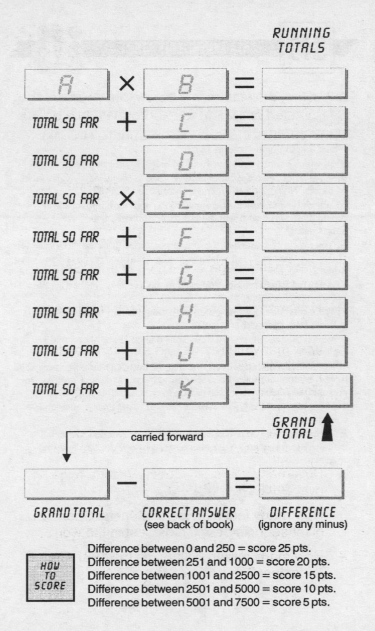

RUNNING TOTALS

| A | × | B | = | |

| TOTAL SO FAR | + | C | = | |

| TOTAL SO FAR | − | D | = | |

| TOTAL SO FAR | × | E | = | |

| TOTAL SO FAR | + | F | = | |

| TOTAL SO FAR | + | G | = | |

| TOTAL SO FAR | − | H | = | |

| TOTAL SO FAR | + | J | = | |

| TOTAL SO FAR | + | K | = | |

GRAND TOTAL ▲

carried forward

| | − | | = | |

GRAND TOTAL / CORRECT ANSWER (see back of book) / DIFFERENCE (ignore any minus)

HOW TO SCORE

Difference between 0 and 250 = score 25 pts.
Difference between 251 and 1000 = score 20 pts.
Difference between 1001 and 2500 = score 15 pts.
Difference between 2501 and 5000 = score 10 pts.
Difference between 5001 and 7500 = score 5 pts.

449

1) What term derives its name from the French for "40 day period" for which animals, people, or vessels are isolated on suspicion of carrying disease?

2) What did Yorgos, a resident on the Greek island of Milos, find whilst digging in his field in 1820?

3) In which country will you find the Sierra Madre mountain range?

4) What letter starts the capital cities of these countries – Afghanistan, Malaysia, Nepal, Sudan, Uganda, Ukraine, and Zaire?

5) Which type of bullet is designed to expand upon impact and is reputedly the type with which President John F. Kennedy was assassinated?

6) You probably know that the kangaroo comes from the Aborigine for "I don't understand", but which animal's Aborigine name is "No drink"?

7) A fax machine is commonly used in modern everyday office life – but what is "fax" short for?

8) What was the nickname given to the famous neurofibromatosis sufferer John Merrick?

9) Which biblical figure had three sons named Ham, Shem, and Japheth?

10) Which vitamin is the only one that the body can manufacture itself, though is more normally obtained through liver and dairy produce, to prevent bone deformation and rickets?

11) Coming from the Greek word *nomisma*, what does a numismatist collect and study?

12) Which tennis trophy has, since 1900, been awarded to the nation with the winning men's team over a series of one doubles and four singles matches?

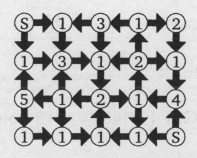

LAP 35

There are no time limits on this lap.

To score each puzzle, refer to the summary on pages 269–270. The maximum scores available are shown below.

	MAX.	SCORE
QUIZWORD	25	
REBUS CHALLENGE	30	
SAFE CRACKER	20	
LOGIC PROBLEM	20	
IN THE PIPELINE	20	
CRIME STORY	25	
WORD ISLAND	30	
MISSING LINKS	30	
NUMEROLOGY	25	
MAGNIFICENT MAZE	25	
TOTAL (max. 250)		

TARGET TO BEAT – 215 points

ACROSS

9   What form of soft gypsum, occurring in England and Italy, can be easily sculpted into figures? (9)

10 Which famous 1938 Evelyn Waugh novel concerned the life of a newspaper reporter? (5)

11 Which Shakespeare play of 1611 tells of a disgruntled duke banished to an island in a storm? (7)

12 What is the term for a contestant on foot taking part in a Spanish *corrida de toros*? (7)

13 In Greek mythology, which monster asked everyone who wished to enter Thebes a riddle? (6)

14 The world's first _____ with a gas light was unveiled in Pall Mall, London on January 29, 1807 (8)

16 Garlic, shallots, asparagus and chives all belong to the common family of which herbaceous flowering plant? (4)

17 What meaty word connects a 1676 rebellion in Virginia, the architect of the Lincoln Memorial, and a 16th Century English philosopher? (5)

18 Which form of Hindu philosophy emphasises the use of bodily control and discipline? (4)

22 What Russian word for "grandmother" is more often used to describe the triangular headscarf commonly worn by such women? (8)

24 To become conscious or break from sleep (4,2)

27 Which class of hunting dog has breeds such as Boston, Border, Scottish, Australian, Irish, Fox and Kerry Blue? (7)

28 Sir Jacob _____, US-born sculptor who settled in England to produce works in Rodin's style, such as *Day and Night* (7)

29 Which American city has a football team called the Dolphins? (5)

30 Which word, associated with food, can be formed from the letters of "GET BARGEE"? (9)

DOWN

1 Which plant has 17 varieties on the endangered species list, including the black-laced, Arizona hedgehog, and silver pincushion? (6)

2 Which famous 17th Century building at Agra, India was built by Shah Jahan as a mausoleum for his wife? (3,5)

3 What is a dramatic performance of an event of local historic interest acted out at a fixed place or on a float in a carnival? (7)

4 Hawaii has been known as the 50th _____ of the USA since August 21, 1959 (5)

5 What is the title of the marching leader who immediately precedes a military band? (4,5)

6 In chemistry, what term describes an atom having the same number of protons but different numbers of neutrons than another atom of the same element? (7)

7 Which Haitian religion idolises a high god called Bon Dieu? (6)

8 What type of musical drama involves a stage play consisting of light-hearted songs and dialogue? (8)

15 Which Scandinavian maidens of Odin are led by Brunhild in a 1856 Wagner opera? (9)

16 Which medical operation removes part of the brain's cortex in order to control behaviour in the patient? (8)

19 Which dish is made from fried beaten eggs usually served with a filling? (8)

20 Which drug, originally obtained from the bark of the willow, has the chemical name acetylsalicylic acid? (7)

21 In Irish legend, what female fairy wails before a family death? (7)

23 What does the "B" stand for in the acronym FBI? (6)

25 What word for a room where food and utensils are kept comes from the Latin word *panitaria*, meaning "bread room"? (6)

26 Which golf club has the largest amount of loft to help the player with shots from a bunker or heavy rough? (5)

_ _ _ _ _ _   _ _ _ _ _ _ _ _

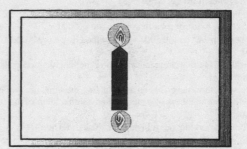

_ _ _ _   _ _ _   _ _ _ _ _ _
_ _   _ _ _ _   _ _ _ _

_ _ _ _ _ _ _ _ _   _ _ _ _ _ _

4

--- ----- ---------

5

--- ---- ---- --------
- -------- -----

6

--- ---- -- ---- --!

Blacken out those segments on the right-hand page that are letter coded to the FALSE statements. This will form a correct mathematical sum.

True False

A   The scientific name for the vulture is *Vulpes vulpes*   ☐☐

B   *Romans* is the penultimate book of the New Testament   ☐☐

C   Thanksgiving Day in the USA falls on the first Thursday in November   ☐☐

D   Spiderman's *alter ego* works as a photographer for the *Daily Bugle*   ☐☐

E   Juno was the Roman King of the gods   ☐☐

F   Zodiac, Prefect and Corsair were models of Audi cars   ☐☐

G   Michelangelo painted the ceiling of the Sistine Chapel   ☐☐

H   The Marx Brothers' real surname was Cooper   ☐☐

J   The first Commandment is "Thou shalt not commit adultery"   ☐☐

K   de Morgan was a famous British mathematician   ☐☐

456

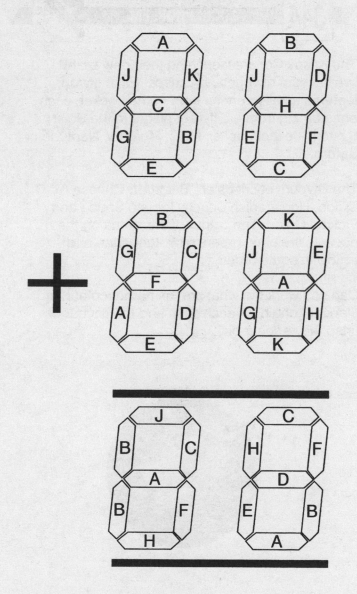

457

344 LOGIC PROBLEM

The Krispy Co. are launching their new brand –
five flavours of vegetarian crisps. Each flavour
features an alien on the front of the packet, each
one coming from a different planet in the Solar
System – either Jupiter, Mars, Mercury, Neptune or
Saturn.

The flavours of crisps are Beetroot, Cheese &
Onion, Horseradish Sauce, Tomato Sauce and
Pickled Onion. The colour of the aliens on the
packets are blue, green, pink, tangerine and
yellow in some order.

Can you work out what are the name, colour and
planet of origin for each alien and the flavour of
crisp they appear on?

CLUES

1. Bungol is pink. He doesn't appear on the Pickled Onion crisp packet nor is he from Jupiter.

2. The Cheese & Onion packet has a blue alien on it.

3. Xippi helps to promote the delicious Horseradish Sauce flavour. He comes from a planet further away from the Sun than the blue alien.

4. Yellow monsters come from Mercury.

5. Kalok and the Tomato Sauce monster live on neighbouring planets of the Solar System.

6. Picked Onion crisps display the Neptune alien, but he is not tangerine coloured.

7. Yterb isn't green.

STARTING HINTS

a. What colour is the monster from Neptune?

b. Find the colour of Jeorj and his flavour of crisps.

c. What flavours do Kalok and Jeorj support?

d. Now look carefully at clues 3 & 5.

Alien	Flavour	Colour	Planet
Bungol			
Jeorj			
Kalok			
Xippi			
Yterb			

Your task is to match the animal characters below with the kind of animals they are. In some cases we give you the book they appear in.

1   Toto in *The Wizard of Oz*

2   Baloo

3   Black Beauty

4   Rosinante in *Don Quixote*

5   Nana in *Peter Pan*

6   Pooh

7   Justice in *Black Beauty*

8   Buck in *Call of the Wild*

9   Kaa

10 Napoleon in *Animal Farm*

11 Flicka in *My Friend Flicka*

12 The Houyhnhnms in *Gulliver's Travels*

13 Snowball

14 Mopsy

15 Polynesia in *Dr. Doolittle*

16 Nag in *The Jungle Book Stories*

17 Lassie

18 Rupert

19 Black Bess in *Rockwood*

20 General Wormwort

IN THE PIPELINE

The best way to demonstrate the In the Pipeline puzzles is to do an example. The rectangular grid shows both ends of three pipes.

1   England
2   Tunisia
3   Greece
4   Mexico
5   Pakistan
6   Colombia
7   Australia
8   Hong Kong
9   New Zealand
10 Libya
11 Cyprus

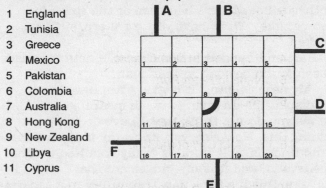

In the full puzzle there would be a list of twenty items on the left (in this case, countries) each of which uses one of the terms below to describe their unit of currency.

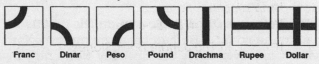

| Franc | Dinar | Peso | Pound | Drachma | Rupee | Dollar |

For each item in the list, draw the appropriate diagram in the numbered square. For example, if question 13 is FRANCE which has the Franc as its currency, draw the symbol corresponding to Franc in box number 13 (as shown above).

261

The Missing Link

Officer Barlow pulled up in his blue Ford outside the house in a depressed, industrial part of the city. Detective Hartland, an ambulance and several other police officers had been at the scene for some time. "What have you got there, sir?" he asked.

Hartland handed him the suicide note that had been found beside the dead man.

"My dear Gillian," it began. "You have been indispensible in giving my life meaning, and I hope you do not think that I have decieved you by doing this. However, you know my independant and unchangable mind is easily comitted to what I believe in, and it is my judgement that I should give up this life for a new tranquility in a separate world from here where debt is not such a burden. I hope that you understand, and that you will not feel embarassed when telling the children. I love you very much, Bennet."

Barlow put the note in a police bag. "Shame. How come he owed so much?"

The Detective filled Barlow in on the details he had found so far. "He had been unemployed for some time, ever since the Bromley News he sub-edited had folded because of falling circulation. He'd been finding it difficult to get a job and he felt he was letting the family down. She was a housewife looking after the children, sometimes helping out at the local hostel. Apart from money troubles, they were seemingly very stable, according to the neighbours I've talked to. Happy marriage, two kids, a model Catholic nuclear family."

"I thought suicide was severely frowned upon by Catholics," said Barlow.

The Detective nodded in agreement. "That's exactly what makes me suspicious. But that's not proof. I think we need something stronger to detect foul play here."

Barlow thought for a moment. "Well, thinking back to my school days, I'm fairly sure the proof is already ours."

Can you spot the exact evidence that provides the extra proof required to suspect murder?

Clues to ten of the longest words that we
managed to find :

1	*e.g. a nuclear weapon?*
2	*Performed, yielded*
3	*One of Santa's helpers*
4	*Pressed the 'TAB' key?*
5	*Offered money for goods*
6	*Buried again*
7	*Wobbled*
8	*Laughed*
9	*Rife*
10	*Main tooth constituent*

464

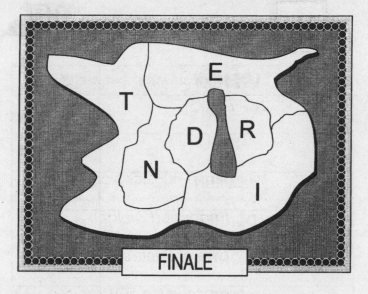

FINALE

Other words of five letters or more (find up to another 20) :

WHO?	GUESSES
NQFZMHRS	12
ANMM	10
EHCDKHN	8
DQNHBZ	6
BNLONRDQ	4
CDZE	2

WHAT?	GUESSES
Z SN E NMD SN YDQN	12
GNTMC CNF EZUNTQHSD	10
RHWSHDR	8
BGNHBD	6
BNHM RKNS	4
LTRHBZK	2

WHERE?	GUESSES
ONQS OQNCTBDQ	**12**
SZFTR	**10**
ZYNQDR	**8**
ZKFZQUD	**6**
BZOHSZK HR KHRANM	**4**
ROZMHRG MDHFGANTQ	**2**

WHEN?	GUESSES
HRKZMC QHRHMF?	**12**
MDV KHED	**10**
GNKHCZX	**8**
RHLMDK	**6**
DFFR	**4**
ATMMX	**2**

For each of the statements below, put your guesstimated answer in the appropriate box on the opposite page.

A   Saturn has the largest number of moons of any planet in the Solar system – how many?

B   How many Oscars did Steven Spielberg's *Schindler's List* win?

C   How many million scouts are there in the USA?

D   How many points are there on the Star of David?

E   On average, how many people live on one square mile of the world's land?

F   How long (in days) is the gestation period of the giraffe?

G   How many cards are there in a standard pack of tarot cards?

H   How many people died of poisoning in the USA in 1992?

J   How many letters are there in the Greek alphabet?

K   How old was William Pitt the Younger when he became Britain's youngest Prime Minister?

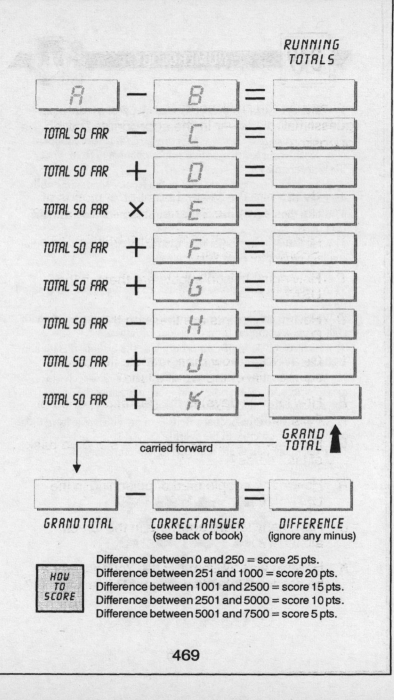

RUNNING TOTALS

$A - B =$

TOTAL SO FAR $- C =$

TOTAL SO FAR $+ D =$

TOTAL SO FAR $\times E =$

TOTAL SO FAR $+ F =$

TOTAL SO FAR $+ G =$

TOTAL SO FAR $- H =$

TOTAL SO FAR $+ J =$

TOTAL SO FAR $+ K =$

GRAND TOTAL

carried forward

GRAND TOTAL $-$ CORRECT ANSWER (see back of book) $=$ DIFFERENCE (ignore any minus)

HOW TO SCORE

Difference between 0 and 250 = score 25 pts.
Difference between 251 and 1000 = score 20 pts.
Difference between 1001 and 2500 = score 15 pts.
Difference between 2501 and 5000 = score 10 pts.
Difference between 5001 and 7500 = score 5 pts.

469

1) Which computer company, formed by punched card pioneer Herman Hollerith, has the simple company motto "Think"?

2) *Rosencrantz and Guildenstern are Dead* is a Tom Stoppard play considering the fate of two minor characters from what Shakespeare play?

3) What connects a natural wind in the Rocky Mountains with the name of a helicopter?

4) Which famous city marks the central point of the Australian land mass?

5) What is the study, sometimes used in forensic science, of the flight of projectiles fired from a weapon?

6) Which is the only airborne mammal?

7) In computing terminology, what does the acronym VDU stand for?

8) Which two colours are most often confused by someone with Daltonism, a common form of colour-blindness?

9) Which Archbishop of Canterbury was the bishop of Bath and Wells before being consecrated in 1991?

10) What natural foodstuff is classified into monosaccharides, disaccharides, trisaccharides, and more unusually the polysaccharides such as cellulose and starch?

11) In what verbal respect are British stamps different from those of every other country in the world?

12) How many points are required to win one game of badminton?

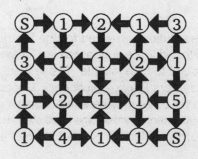

NOTE – the solutions provided for the Word Island puzzles in Round 2 are suggested lists of words that our computer found to be available. These were checked against *Chambers English Dictionary*. Depending upon where you live, there may be some words that you have found in your dictionary that are not listed herein. By all means, award yourself the points for these words.

251. **ACROSS: 1** *Apocalypse Now*, **8** Knossos, **9** Preview, **11** Loofah, **13** Yearlong, **15** Manes, **16** Orpheus, **18** Baptist, **19** Lamia, **21** Aversion, **23** Italic, **25** Outpost, **26** Two-step, **28** Hercule Poirot.
DOWN: 2 Pronoun, **3** Cos, **4** Lisp, **5** Pepperpots, **6** Emeer, **7** Ominous, **8** Kilimanjaro, **10** Wightman Cup, **12** Aesop, **14** Horizontal, **17** Eclat, **18** Breathe, **20** Mulatto, **22** Stoic, **24** Stop, **27** Oui.

252. 1) Blood is thicker than water, 2) Talk turkey, 3) Once in a blue moon, 4) The Industrial Revolution, 5) Two left feet, 6) Third degree burn.

253. True statements are A, B, G, K. False statements (with corrections in brackets) are C (Psalms has the most), D (Ontario and Toronto are transposed), E (Upper Volta), F (Terpsichore), H (St Christopher), J (Olympia). The sum formed is 54 + 37 = 91.

254. Full solution on page 474. Summary given here :

Dan	Jill	New Inn pub	7pm
Dave	Jane	Cinema	9pm
David	Katherine	Rixy's nightclub	11pm
Patrick	Victoria	Watched video	10pm
Simon	Mary	Ice skating	8pm

255. A connects to D; B connects to E; C connects to F.

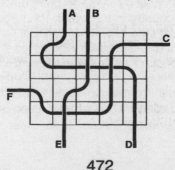

256. Although there are lots of ways in which the criminal's story could be false, the following are definite factual errors. Firstly, Irving Berlin could not read nor write music using scores. Second, Leonardo da Vinci wrote in mirror writing which could hardly be described as "clear Italian". Finally, the *Mona Lisa* is painted on wood, not canvas, and so could not have been rolled up into a tube. Spotting any two of these three earns the points.

257. 92 words. Clued words : soonest detested entente stetson détente oneness denotes sonnets settees noosed. Unclued words : deeded denes denned denote denoted dented dents detent détentes detents detest detests dodos donee donees donned dosed doses dossed dosses doted dotes dotted ententes needed nested nests netted nodded nodes nodose nones noose noosed nooses nosed noses noted notes oddest seeded sennet sestet sestets seton setose settee sodded sodden sones sonnet steed stenos stenosed stenoses stetted stone stoned stones stood tedded tenet tenets tenon tented tents teste tested testes tests toned tones tonne tonnes tooted toots tossed tosses toted totes totted tsetse tsetses.

258. (**These answers include notes explaining the more obscure clues**) WHO? = George Bush (who was head of the CIA before becoming the 41st President). WHAT? = Compact Disc. WHERE? = Australia (everyone is compelled to vote = "compulsory suffrage"; it is the flattest country in the world; Paul Keating is the Prime Minister, at time of writing). WHEN? = The Gunpowder Plot (the Catholic revolt against James I, led by Catesby although Fawkes was the one who was caught).

259. A=18, B=5, C=16, D=32, E=42, F=5, G=22, H=12, J=55, K=71, ANSWER=1067.

260. The correct answers are : 1) *E.T.,* 2) Little dots, 3) Israel, 4) Pangaea, 5) Sword, 6) Bark, 7) Facsimile, 8) Heart, 9) Castor and Pollux, 10) Carat, 11) History, 12) Archery.

FULL SOLUTION TO LOGIC PROBLEM, PUZZLE 254

(a) Mary went skating at 7pm or 8pm (clue 2) but the 7pm is the New Inn date (clue 3) so she must have gone at 8pm with Simon (clue 6). Jane could not have gone to the New Inn at 7pm since she went out an hour before Patrick and Victoria (clues 4 & 7) who did not go out at 8pm since we already know Mary and Simon went out then. Katherine went out at 11pm (clue 1), meaning it must have been Jill who went out to the New Inn at 7pm.

(b) Patrick and Victoria did not go out at 8pm [when we know Simon when out] or 11pm [because Katherine went out then] or 7pm [when we know Jill went out]. So they must have gone out at 9pm or 10pm. Similarly, Jane went out at 9pm or 10pm since we know Jill went out at 7pm, Mary went out at 8pm, and Katherine went out at 11pm. Using clue 7 we deduce that Jane went out at 9pm and Patrick went out at 10pm. This leaves Victoria, who must have gone out at 10pm.

(c) Dan isn't going out with Jane (clue 9), Katherine (clue 1), Mary [we know she is seeing Simon] or Victoria [who is seeing Patrick] so Dan must be with Jill.

So far the situation is :

Man	Woman	Venue	Time
Dan	Jill	New Inn pub	7pm
Dave	???	???	???
David	???	Rixy's night-club	???
Patrick	Victoria	???	10pm
Simon	Mary	Ice Skating	8pm

The video wasn't at 11pm (clue 8), 7pm (clue 3), 8pm [the ice-skating time], or 9pm [since Jane went out then but she didn't see the video by clue 7] so it must have been at 10pm with Patrick and Victoria, leaving Dave and his date to go to the cinema – the only remaining venue.

As Katherine didn't go to the cinema (clue 1), she must be the other night-clubber, and Jane must have gone to the movies with Dave at 9pm. David and Kath must have gone to Rixy's at 11pm, the only remaining time-slot. And that's all there is to it!

261. **ACROSS: 1** Willow pattern, **8** Deplete, **9** Proverb, **11** V-Necks, **13** Maverick, **15** Laser, **16** Premium, **18** Ravioli, **19** Ideal, **21** Inscribe, **23** Emboss, **25** Natural, **26** Czarina, **28** Down's syndrome.
DOWN: 2 Impress, **3** Lee, **4** Wren, **5** Alphabetic, **6** Those, **7** Rhenium, **8** Devaluation, **10** Baked Alaska, **12** Kirov, **14** Spoonbills, **17** Idiom, **18** Risotto, **20** Egotism, **22** Rerun, **24** Icon, **27** APR.

262. 1) Hot under the collar, 2) The third dimension, 3) Splitting hairs (sounds like "hares"), 4) Every now and then, 5) Saw the funny side, 6) Short term memory.

263. True statements are D, F, G. False statements are A (Mozart), B (Corinthian), C (11th Century), E (Peso), H (St Matthew), J (Athens), K (Harvard). The sum formed is $80 - 54 = 26$.

264.

Peg 1	Eve	Polo neck	Tan
Peg 2	Clare	Anorak	Brown
Peg 3	Bernard	Raincoat	Black
Peg 4	Dominic	Cardigan	Blue
Peg 5	Adrian	Duffel coat	Green

265. A connects to E; B connects to F; C connects to D.

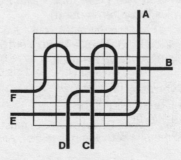

266. In 1962, the *Mariner I* mission was launched towards Venus. However, the rocket separated from the boosters too soon and plunged into the ocean just four minutes after take-off. The cause? A missing minus sign ("a short, horizontal line") from the computer program, caused by human error.

267. 62 words.
Clued words : nineteen tontine retinite reenter tenner torrent trotter titter terrene retorter.
Unclued words : entente enter enterer enteron error inert inner intent inter intine intone intoner intro intron ninon nitre otter renin rennet rennin renter retene retort retro rooter rotenone rotor rotten rottener rotter teeter tenet tenon tenor tenter terete terret terror tetter tinner tinter titre toner tonne tontiner tooter torte torten totter totterer treen.

268. WHO? = Archimedes (he invented the Archimedes Screw; clue 3 refers to his discovery of pi; clue 4 refers to his problem of finding out whether the king's crown was made from real gold).
WHAT? = A piano (whose full name of pianoforte means "quiet loud" in French; clue 4 lists the black and white layout of one octave; Steinway is a famous make of piano).
WHERE? = Madame Tussaud's (which is in the same building as the London Laserium).
WHEN? = The Gulf War (*Tomahawk* and *Patriot* were the principal missile systems used).

269. A=14, B=20, C=95, D=35, E=60, F=161, G=76, H=9, J=12, K=28, ANSWER=2068.

270. The answers are :
    1) Sir Christopher Wren
    2) *The World*
    3) Bay Of Biscay

4) Snow
5) Tricolours
6) Jupiter
7) Sulphur
8) Rhombus
9) Valhalla
10) (Used) Car Salesman
11) Orange
12) Harold Lloyd

271. **ACROSS: 8** Creamery, **9** Ureter, **10** Step-sister, **11** Acid, **12** Proper, **14** Ricochet, **15** Quartet, **17** Aphasia, **20** Hologram, **22** Norton, **24** Kiwi, **25** Salamander, **27** In-laws, **28** Atropine.
DOWN: 1 Crater, **2** Carp, **3** Pedigree, **4** Mystery, **5** Rubric, **6** Sedan-chair, **7** Beriberi, **13** Periodical, **16** Utopians, **18** Penumbra, **19** Amalgam, **21** Resist, **23** Oceans, **26** Nape.

272. 1) Fatal Attraction, 2) Commercial break, 3) Cuts both ways, 4) Open and shut case, 5) Tom, Dick and Harry (the pictures are of Tom Hanks, Richard Nixon and Harry Belafonte), 6) Point blank range (a decimal point, then a blank, then a range of mountains).

273. True statements are A, D, E, F, K. False statements are B (domed roof on a square tower), C (Spanish Inquisition), G (mournfully), H (crowds), J (frequency). The sum formed is 17 x 4 = 68.

274.

Row 1	Column D	Stock-car race	$25,000
Row 2	Column B	Dog walker	$10,000
Row 3	Column E	Custard pie	$1,000
Row 4	Column C	Wrestling	$5,000
Row 5	Column A	Donate $100	$2,000

275. A connects to B; C connects to E; D connects to F.

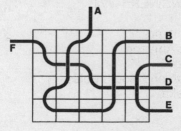

276. "Direct flights" between two places of different latitude over a spherical surface such as the Earth's usually look curved when projected on to flat maps. Therefore, the pilot could not have plotted the flight plan using "a pencil and ruler".

277. 54 words.
Clued words : decider receded derided decree ridded derriere reeled deicide leered eerie.
Unclued words : ceded ceiled celled cerci cered cider cirri creed creel cried crier decide decided decreed decried decrier deeded deled deride derider diced dicer dicier direr eddied eerier eider elide elided erred icier leerier lidded lieder recede redder redid reedier reeler relic relied ridder rider riled.

278. WHO? = William Shakespeare (who spelled his name many different ways; he married Anne Hathaway).
WHAT? = Diamond (the hardest naturally occuring substance at 10 on the Mohs' scale of hardness; Brilliant and Rose are cuts of diamond).
WHERE? = Buckingham Palace (it has a fountain outside it; in 1825, its front was rebuilt by John Nash; it is situated on the Mall in London).
WHEN? = Assassination of John F. Kennedy (Earl Warren was the Chief Justice who led the enquiry to investigate whether the murder was a conspiracy; Lee Harvey Oswald was killed by Jack Ruby).

279. A=20, B=7, C=4, D=26, E=9, F=4, G=385, H=6, J=64, K=46, ANSWER=1771.

280. The anwers are :
     1) The Amazon
     2) Mozart
     3) North and South Poles
     4) Alaska
     5) Tail

6) Uranium, Plutonium, Mercury
7) All their sides have the same length
8) Harpies
9) Ouija Board
10) All have been vice-presidents
11) *Cluedo*
12) Seven (the Heptathlon)

281. **ACROSS: 8** Crowfoot, **9** Phobia, **10** Adam's apple, **11** Lapp, **12** Crisis, **14** Nepotism, **15** Fascism, **17** Columns, **20** Cephalic, **22** Thebes, **24** Star, **25** Abbreviate, **27** Bronze, **28** Richmond.
DOWN: 1 Trader, **2** Swim, **3** Molasses, **4** Stipend, **5** Upkeep, **6** Cos lettuce, **7** Diapason, **13** Saccharine, **16** Aperture, **18** Outreach, **19** Iceberg, **21** Loaves, **23** Extant, **26** Iamb.

282. 1) Centre of gravity, 2) Coffee table book, 3) The long and short of it, 4) Shorthand typist, 5) The League of Nations, 6) Miss the bus.

283. True statements are A, D, J, K. False statements are B (throat and neck), C (All the Love in the World), E (Nile), F (1852), G (yes he did, in 1954), H (men). The sum formed is 16 + 37 = 53.

284.

Aardvark	Trevor	Gossip	Wednesday
Badger	Peter	Evening News	Friday
Fish	Simone	Times	Monday
Snake	Lucy	Post	Tuesday
Yak	Millie	Press	Thursday

285. A connects to E; B connects to F; C connects to D.

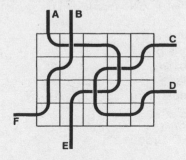

481

286. If you didn't spot this one, get ready to groan. Earlier in the story you are told that the man thought the pilot was a friend of his, Jack Delaney. When the man on the aeroplane got up, he knocked on the door and said "Hi, Jack!"...

287. 40 words.
Clued words : macramé mamma creamier camera crammer arrear merrier acacia carrier maraca.
Unclued words : acari aerie airier career carer circa cirri cream creamer creme crier crime eerie eerier emmer erica icier mammae maria marrier mimer mimic mirier racier ramie rarer reamer rearer rimae rimer.

288. WHO? = Fred Flintstone (Bedrock is his home town).
WHAT? = The Eiffel Tower (originally built on the Champ de Mars for the 1889 Paris Exhibition; in World War I, it was used as a look-out post because at the time it was one of the highest buildings in the world).
WHERE? = Pyramid (a ziggurat is a stepped-side pyramid; Cheops is buried in the Great Pyramid at Giza).
WHEN? = The Irangate affair (*Hawk* was the name of the missiles in question; other clues refer to evidence that was allegedly shredded by Oliver North's secretary).

289. A=13, B=10, C=50, D=27, E=29, F=66, G=88, H=107, J=23, K=57, ANSWER=3711.

290. The answers are :
        1) James Bond
        2) Michigan
        3) Canada
        4) Crimean War
        5) Racing
        6) Polymer
        7) The O Group

8) Tarot Cards
9) Georgio Armani
10) Mah Jong
11) 400 metres
12) Disqualification

291. **ACROSS: 8** Motion, **9** El Dorado, **10** Waterwheel, **11** Vein, **12** Ebb tide, **14** Eclair, **15** Midgets, **17** Sailing, **20** Rector, **22** One-step, **24** Pier, **25** Absolution, **27** End users, **28** Fiddle.
DOWN: 1 Potage, **2** Mixed bag, **3** Snow, **4** Referee, **5** Adulterate, **6** Gravel, **7** Addition, **13** Interfaces, **16** Iberians, **18** Latitude, **19** Possess, **21** Torque, **23** Poodle, **26** Left.

292. 1) Double Your Money, 2) A word in edgeways, 3) Rip Van Winkle, 4) Cat's eyes, 5) Innocents Abroad, 6) Race against time.

293. True statements are B, D, F, G. False statements are A (Brazil), C (four), E (London and Paris), H (Mars), J (sternum), K (Virgo). The sum formed is 94 − 10 = 84.

294.

Debbie	Collingwood	Margherita	8pm
Heather	Aidan's	Pepperoni	8.30pm
Ian	Van Mildert	Anchovies	10.30pm
Kay	Trevelyan	Hot & Spicy	7.15pm
Martin	Grey	Fuengerola	9.15pm

295. A connects to E; B connects to D; C connects to F.

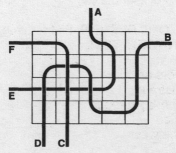

484

296. The builder was clearly lying. He had been "the one working on that floor", and he said himself that the scene was as the detectives first saw it. The man then "opened the door" – impossible, since the woman could not have closed the door behind her since there was no floor on the other side.

297. 63 words.
Clued words : goddess dodged detested oddest stodge stooge dotted sedge totted seeded.
Unclued words : deeded detest detests dodge dodged dodges dodos doges dogged doggo dosed doses dossed dosses doted dotes edged edges egest egests egged geese gesso goddesses godet godets goose goosed goosegog gooses sedges sestet sestets setose settee settees sodded steed stetted stood stooges teste tested testes tests togged tooted toots tossed tosses toted totes tsetse tsetses.

298. WHO? = Woody Allen (real name Allen Konigsberg).
WHAT? = Typewriter (first commercially made by Remington before the popular IBM 72 emerged).
WHERE? = Rome (capital of the Lazio region; site of the signing of various famous treaties).
WHEN? = First Men on the Moon (clue 1 refers to the fact that the walk was a long way away!; clue 2 refers to the telephone call to President Nixon; the landing was made in the Sea of Tranquillity).

299. A=5, B=3, C=8, D=8, E=6, F=14, G=66, H=213, J=93, K=41, ANSWER=7283.

300. The answers are:
　　　1) Balustrade
　　　2) *Pilgrim's Progress*
　　　3) Mexico
　　　4) To the west

5) Blue
6) Edwin Hubble
7) Hydrogen
8) Ruby
9) Two
10) Detects lies
11) Tea
12) Hammer

301. **ACROSS: 8** Melody, **9** Aardvark, **10** Statute-law, **11** Tito, **12** Reactor, **14** Lyrics, **15** Earlobe, **17** Pitfall, **20** Dowser, **22** Ragweed, **24** *Very*, **25** Addis Ababa, **27** Catholic, **28** Cuckoo.
DOWN: 1 Vector, **2** Football, **3** Cyst, **4** Mallard, **5** Arc-welding, **6** Avatar, **7** Critical, **13** Tabernacle, **16** Above par, **18** Feedback, **19** Art Deco, **21** Scythe, **23** Debtor, **26** Sect.

302. 1) Acid rain, 2) Russian roulette, 3) Perpetual motion, 4) Pure mathematics, 5) California Girls, 6) Latter Day Saints.

303. True statements are C, D, H, K. False statements are A (Netherlands), B (seven), E (plain green rectangle), F (trombone), G (Verdi), J (seven). The sum formed is 27 x 3 = 81.

304.

Graham	Everett	Purple	Celebrities
James	Kendal	Grey	Books
John	Sanders	Orange	TV
Patrick	Erwin	Blue	Music
Paul	Harper	Green	Films

305. A connects to C; B connects to F; D connects to E.

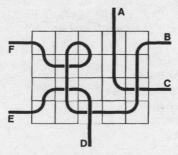

306. There were two drivers travelling in opposite directions in dense fog, which affects visibility through windscreens badly, despite the windscreen wipers. They had both put their heads out of their side windows simultaneously and their heads clashed, resulting in bad head injuries. The cars came to a gradual stop some yards later. This explains the unharmed cars still having their engines running.

307. 39 words.
Clued words : imitate maimed dimmed immediate mediated meditate dimidiate mimetite emitted deemed.
Unclued words : aided aimed amide deeded demit demitted edema edited imamate imide imitated mamma mated matte matted media mediate medii meditated meted mimed tamed tatami tatted tedded teemed tided timed timid.

308. WHO? = Charles Dickens (used pen-name of Boz; his stories were first serialised when published).
WHAT? = Cornflakes (originally designed as a food for hospital patients, it was then sold via mail order; the famous Kellogg signature is still seen on packets today).
WHERE? = Oxford University (home of the *Oxford English Dictionary*).
WHEN? = The Boston Tea Party (the tea was owned by the East India Company; clue 6 is a slightly cryptic reference to the Mad Hatter's Tea Party in *Alice in Wonderland*).

309. A=6, B=76, C=8, D=195, E=300, F=12, G=28, H=88, J=80, K=12, ANSWER=2116.

310. The answers are :
     1) Silver bullet
     2) Christine Brinkley
     3) Argentina
     4) Jamaica
     5) Legion

6) Chlorophyll
7) London Bridge
8) Microwave oven
9) Lee Harvey Oswald
10) Bordeaux
11) Discus (1kg and 2kg)
12) Polo

311. **ACROSS: 1** Demerara, **5** Tandem, **10** Backspace, **11** Minor, **12** Orwell, **13** Odysseus, **15** Horsehair, **17** Nine, **20** Clef, **21** Marshland, **24** Maharaja, **25** Advent, **28** Thumb, **29** Cabriolet, **30** Reeves, **31** Kedgeree. **DOWN: 1** Debtor, **2** Macaw, **3** Restless, **4** Ream, **6** Almost, **7** Dandelion, **8** Marksmen, **9** Head first, **14** Cheap-jack, **16** Open house, **18** Scimitar, **19** Cladding, **22** Treble, **23** Statue, **26** Euler, **27** Oboe.

312. 1) Split infinitive, 2) Shooting gallery, 3) Raise the alarm, 4) Vulgar fraction, 5) Chicken Maryland, 6) Vertical take-off.

313. True statements are C, D, E, H. False statements are A (Laz Paz), B (Red Sox), F (Anise), G (had one opera), J (Sputnik 2), K (polyglot). The sum formed is 13 + 26 = 39.

314.

Picture A	Freaky Fred	Poaching	3 years
Picture B	Cad Clive	Treason	15 years
Picture C	Tough Tim	Rustling	7 years
Picture D	Bruiser Bill	Deception	10 years
Picture E	Slippery Sam	Forgery	6 years

315. A connects to F; B connects to D; C connects to E.

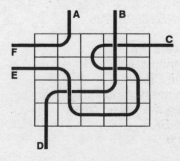

316. Among the duty-free goods the bee-keeper received was some cologne. He wore some the next day and the bees did not recognise his scent, and so they attacked the 'stranger' to their hive. When the Inspector went into the closed space of the ambulance he could smell the cologne.

317. 42 words.
Clued words : useless sublessee pulseless bubbles pebble epees sleeps blesses belle peepul.
Unclued words : beeps belles bells bleep bleeps bless bubble bulbul bulbuls bulls buses busses lessee lessees lulls lupus pebbles peels peeps pubes pules pulls pulse pulses seels seeps sells sepses sleep speel spell spells.

318. WHO? = Leonardo da Vinci (who wrote in mirror writing, as we know from Lap 26!; he painted the *Last Supper* and designed the first helicopter).
WHAT? = Cash/Credit Card (Diner's Club was the first credit card to be introduced).
WHERE? = The Andes (they are a large mountain system, or cordillera, near Cape Horn; highest peak is Aconcagua, and Titicaca is the highest lake in the world).
WHEN? = The Olympic Games (there were no Olympics in 1914, 1940 or 1944 due to wars; the flag with five rings represents the continents).

319. A=12, B=4, C=22, D=6, E=92, F=13, G=69, H=25, J=11, K=20, ANSWER=1236.

320. The answers are :
      1) Mathematics
      2) John Cleese
      3) It is not rectangular
      4) They are walled cities
      5) The SAS
      6) Wine

7) Doesn't stick to a magnet
8) Troposphere
9) All are Holy Books
10) Angostura Bitters
11) Three
12) *Americas' Cup*

321. **ACROSS: 1** Chaplain, **5** I.D. card, **10** Baby teeth, **11** Omega, **12** Energy, **13** Ice skate, **15** Clingfilm, **17** Edge, **20** Cube, **21** Pentagram, **24** Corvette, **25** Iguana, **28** Ecole, **29** Viscosity, **30** Muscat, **31** Leap year. **DOWN: 1** Cobweb, **2** Amble, **3** Litigant, **4** Ibex, **6** Dropsy, **7** Alexandra, **8** Diameter, **9** Chocolate, **14** Effective, **16** Laborious, **18** Ice cream, **19** Age group, **22** Peseta, **23** Lawyer, **26** Alice, **27** Isle.

322. 1) Swinging Sixties, 2) Waste not, want not, 3) Six of one and half a dozen of another, 4) Burn the midnight oil, 5) Vitamin B complex (anagram of "Vitamin B"), 6) Peak viewing time.

323. True statements are D, G, J. False statements are A (5th), B (140 British, 4000 Zulus), C ('89), E (speaking aloud), F (onomatopoeia), H (Spencer Percival was), K (broad and slow). The sum formed is 96 – 69 = 27.

324.

Annabel	Personnel	Level 4	Level 5
Jonathan	Data Processing	Level 1	Level 4
Melanie	Purchasing	Level 2	Level 1
Norman	Accounts	Level 5	Level 3
Steve	Marketing	Level 3	Level 2

325. A connects to C; B connects to F; D connects to E.

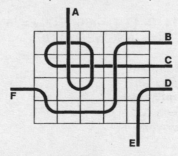

493

`326. The man had no trouble reading the Arabic numbers (1, 2, 5, etc.) on the coins of most Western countries. However, he was currently in the United States which has words on its coins (such as TEN CENTS) which the Arab could not read. Hence, he had to guess what coins to put into the machine to make it work. It did not work if he put too much in since it accepted the exact coins only.

327. 47 words.
Clued words : tattooists cassata statistics static staccato cocoa otitis cacao assists cassis.
Unclued words : ascitic ascot ascots assist assists astatic attics casts cists coast coasts coati coatis coats cocci coots cotta iotas oasis otitic scats scoot scoots stasis statics statist statistic stats stoat stoic stoics tacit tattoo tattooist titis toast toasts.

328. WHO? = Garfield the cat.
WHAT? = The planet Mars (whose atmosphere is almost entirely made up of Carbon Dioxide; its year is 687 Earth days long; Phobos and Deimos are its moons; it is the fourth planet of the Solar System).
WHERE? = New York City (built on the junction of the Hudson and East rivers; was once capital of the USA; Staten Island is one of its boroughs).
WHEN? = The Soccer World Cup (was held in the USA in 1994; FIFA is the international ruling body; the original Jules Rimet trophy was kept by Brazil in 1970 who had it three times).

329. A=7, B=14, C=12, D=460, E=3, F=75, G=88, H=206, J=167, K=6, ANSWER=4378.

330. The answers are:
     1) *Peter Pan*
     2) Court Jesters
     3) Seven
     4) New York

5) Spain
6) Puma
7) Carburettor
8) *Aurora Borealis*
9) Roman Catholicism
10) Cayenne
11) Cheese
12) Three

331. **ACROSS: 9** Oast-house, **10** Amigo, **11** Reactor, **12** Each way, **13** Eggnog, **14** Glycerol, **16** Rite, **17** Dodge, **18** East, **22** Nebraska, **24** Parrot, **27** Embassy, **28** Le Havre, **29** U-Boat, **30** Unnatural.
DOWN: 1 Bourse, **2** Escargot, **3** Ghettos, **4** Curry, **5** Genealogy, **6** Paycock, **7** Viewer, **8** Polyglot, **15** Monkey-nut, **16** Runner-up, **19** Aardvark, **20** Bassets, **21** Machete, **23** Baboon, **25** Treble, **26** Plank.

332. 1) Top Cat, 2) Wall Street crash, 3) Make a night of it, 4) The Silence of the Lambs, 5) Foreign exchange, 6) Around the World in 80 Days.

333. True statements are A, C, F, J. False statements are B (73 mph), D (parliament), E (pineapple), G (Paul Cezanne), H (Yankee), K (pantograph). The sum formed is 13 x 6 = 78.

334.

Picture A	Theresa	Earl Shilton	Cor anglais
Picture B	Paula	Narborough	Flute
Picture C	Rhona	Countesthorpe	Trumpet
Picture D	Olivia	Wigston	Bassoon
Picture E	Sandra	Broughton Ast.	Saxophone

335. A connects to D; B connects to C; E connects to F.

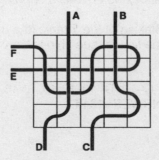

496

336. The Inspector had assumed the case was a typical terrorist attack and that the woman had been carrying a bomb in a plastic bag. The woman had been smuggling in drugs from Cuba. She was "carrying" a plastic bag full of drugs in her stomach. The bag burst, releasing the huge amount of drugs into her bloodstream causing her to "go berserk" (as Penny had said at the start of the story) then die.

337. 81 words.
Clued words : tartar iterate reiterate aggregate regretter arrearage greegree titrate retreat regatta.
Unclued words : aerate aerie agate agree arete arietta arrear arret artier attar attire eager eagre eatage eerie eerier egger egret errata etagere etrier garage garget garret garter getter grate grater greater greet greeter gritter grittier irate irritate rater ratite ratter rattier rearer regear reggae regrate regrater regret reiter retie retire tagger target tarrier tarter tartrate tatter tattier tearer teeter terata terete terra terrae terret terrier tetra tetter titre titter treater trier trite triter.

338. WHO? = Albert Einstein (whose name literally means "beer mug" in German).
WHAT? = The Statue of Liberty (designed by Auguste Bartholdi; one is in New York Harbour, a smaller repilca is in France).
WHERE? = France (Massif Central is a large range of mountains in France; the Loire is a famous French river).
WHEN? = The Sinking of the *Titanic* (the captain was Edward Smith; the first rescue ship to arrive was the *Carpathia*).

339. A=4, B=10, C=70, D=18, E=10, F=46, G=89, H=63, J=275, K=47, ANSWER=1314.

340. The answers are:
1) Quarantine
2) *Venus De Milo*
3) Mexico
4) K
5) Dum Dum
6) Koala
7) Facsimile
8) The Elephant Man
9) Noah
10) Vitamin D
11) Coins
12) The Davis Cup

341. **ACROSS: 9** Alabaster, **10** Scoop, **11** Tempest, **12** Matador, **13** Sphinx, **14** Lamppost, **16** Lily, **17** Bacon, **18** Yoga, **22** Babushka, **24** Wake up, **27** Terrier, **28** Epstein, **29** Miami, **30** Eggbeater.
DOWN: 1 Cactus, **2** Taj Mahal, **3** Pageant, **4** State, **5** Drum major, **6** Isotope, **7** Voodoo, **8** Operetta, **15** Valkyries, **16** Lobotomy, **19** Omelette, **20** Aspirin, **21** Banshee, **23** Bureau, **25** Pantry, **26** Wedge.

342. 1) Record breaking, 2) Burn the candle at both ends, 3) Pineapple chunks, 4) The final countdown, 5) The face that launched a thousand ships (the Queen launches Commonwealth ships) 6) Not much to look at!

343. True statements are D, G, K. False statements are A (fox), B (6th book), C (fourth), E (was Roman Queen!), F (Ford), H (it *is* Marx), J ("Thou shalt have no other gods before me"). The sum formed is 56 + 24 = 80.

344.

Bungol	Tomato sauce	Pink	Mars
Jeorj	Pickled onion	Green	Neptune
Kalok	Cheese & onion	Blue	Jupiter
Xippi	Horseradish	Tangerine	Saturn
Yterb	Beetroot	Yellow	Mercury

345. A connects to F; B connects to E; C connects to D.

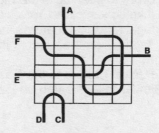

346. This was certainly murder. Although Bennet had been working as a newspaper sub-editor for many years, no less than eight words (indispensable, deceived, independent, unchangeable, committed, tranquillity, separate, embarrassed) are incorrectly spelled out on the suicide note. Obviously the murderer had tried to be more poetic than he was capable of being.

347. 118 words.
Clued words : deterrent rendered reindeer indented tendered reinterred teetered tittered ridden dentine. Unclued words : deeded denied denier denned dented dentin deride derided derider derriere detent détente deter deterred diene dieted dieter diner dinette dinned dinner direr dited eerie eerier eider ended entente enter entered enterer entire indeed indene indent indenter inedited inner intend intended intender intent inter interred intine needed needer needier netted nineteen nittier redden reddened redder reedier reenter reentered reined reinter reiter rended render renderer renin rennet rennin rented renter retene retie retied retinite retire retired ridded ridder rider tedded tedder teenier teeter tended tender tenderer tenet tenner tented tenter terrene terret terrier terrine tetter tided tidied tidier tiered tinder tined tineid tinier tinned tinner tinnier tinted tinter tired titter.

348. WHO? = Beethoven (he became a royal organist at Bonn; composed *Eroica* and *Fidelio*).
WHAT? = Juke Box (*Hound Dog* is the most widely played track on juke boxes; clue 1 refers to the buttons).
WHERE? = Portugal (physical features include the Azores and the Tagus river; the Algarve is a famous Portguese region).
WHEN? = Easter (clue 1 refers to the Easter Rising and Easter Island; Simnel cake is eaten on Easter Sunday).

349. A=18, B=7, C=5, D=6, E=41, F=460, G=78, H=13, J=24, K=24, ANSWER=1065.

350. The answers are:
1) IBM
2) *Hamlet*
3) Chinook
4) Alice Springs
5) Ballistics
6) Bat
7) Visual Display Unit
8) Red and green
9) Dr. George Carey
10) Sugar
11) Does not give country of origin on its stamps
12) Fifteen

ROUND 2 PROGRESS CHART

Plot your score on the chart and see if you are keeping up with the target to beat.

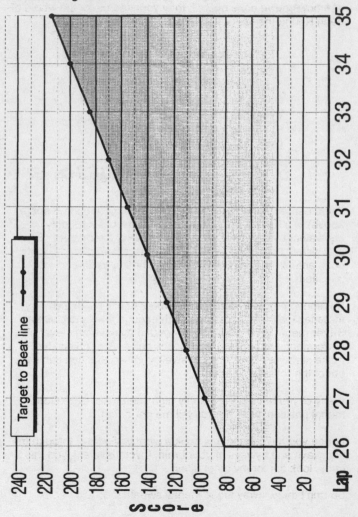

502

THE FINAL RECKONING

How have you found the going? Did the graphs reveal that your scores improved as you progressed through the book? To see how you've done overall, total your scores for the whole of each Round then refer to the medal table below :

	ROUND 1	ROUND 2
G	*480*	*1900*
S	*340*	*1450*
B	*215*	*1000*

If you earned enough points for a **Bronze** medal (the B scores above) in a Round, congratulations! This level is roughly equivalent to answering the easiest 50% of the puzzles completely correctly – no mean feat, considering "easy" in this book actually means "less hard than the impossible questions"!

Seasoned puzzlers, who may be more familiar with the material, may find themselves with enough points to claim a **Silver** medal. If so, well done! To attain this average level of performance throughout the book is quite outstanding. Just make sure your head doesn't swell so much that you can't get out of the room.

If any of you have a sickeningly high score above the **Gold** medal position, well... words fail me (for once).

I hope you have found this book a worthwhile trawl through the highways and byways of your brain. If you have enjoyed this book, look out for my other titles.

So don't throw away those mental sweatbands just yet...

ACKNOWLEDGEMENTS

Copyright clipart used in this book originates from the following companies : 3G Graphics Inc., Archive Arts, BBL Typographic, Cartesia Software, Corel Corporation, Image Club Graphics Inc., Management Graphics Ltd., One Mile Up Inc., Studio Piazza Xilo M.C., Techpool Studios Inc., Totem Graphics Inc., TNT Designs.

Book layout by David J. Bodycombe at *Labyrinth Games* using *CorelDraw!* 5, © Corel Corporation 1994.

All events depicted in this book, including the Mystery Stories, are intended as fictitious and any resemblance to any event or legal case, past or present, is purely coincidental.

The author would like to thank:

Chris Dickson for many constructive criticisms of the first draft, suggesting some good puzzles, and helping me "brainstorm" for new ideas.

Jane MacKenzie, Patrick Erwin, Daniel Connolly, and Mary Deliyannis for testing some of the puzzles.

All the staff at *Robinson Publishing*.

My friends for their supportive curiosity.

My parents, Sheila and David, who have helped with testing ideas or looking up curious information for a long time.